Sport Fishing

and

Aquatic Resources Handbook

Authored by
Bob Schmidt

Graphics by
John Rice

Editor
Louis R. Jensen, Ed.D.

Associate Editor
Sharon Rushton

 KENDALL/HUNT PUBLISHING COMPANY
2460 Kerper Boulevard P.O. Box 539 Dubuque, Iowa 52004-0539

ABOUT THE AUTHOR

Bob Schmidt is a freelance outdoor writer residing in Chicago. He was the first editor of *In-Fisherman Magazine* and then worked fourteen years as a writer and editor in educational publications for elementary school through junior college students. He has been a full-time freelance outdoor writer since 1982, writing three books and one booklet on fishing for the Boy Scouts of America, and contributing articles to outdoor magazines and writing for consumer and trade publications. He is a graduate of the Marquette University College of Journalism and past president of the Association of Great Lakes Outdoor Writers.

ABOUT THE GRAPHIC ARTIST

John Rice is a freelance illustrator residing in New York City. He is a frequent contributor to Field & Stream magazine and his drawings appear in McClaine's Game Fish of North America. He had his first one-man show in 1985 and his artwork has been auctioned for Trout and Ducks Unlimited. He is a graduate of Visual and Performing Arts, Syracuse University.

This edition has been printed directly from camera-ready copy.

Copyright © 1991 by American Fishing Tackle Manufacturer's Association

AFTMA Special Printing

Printed in the United States of America
10 9 8 7 6 5 4 3 2 1

TABLE OF CONTENTS

PREFACE

It is very important to give our children proper recreation that will not only entertain them for now but will enlighten them throughout their lives.

Today's world is full of distractions which take away from families being together and spending good quality time with each other. One of the biggest problems facing our children today is drug abuse. We, as parents and adults, must take an active interest in our children's behavior. We must provide the support and guidance which are needed to resist drugs. We are the role models for our children. Our life styles and attitudes will be copied by future generations. It is up to us to make the difference today and set the proper examples of right and wrong.

A great way to improve family communication is involvement in fishing. Fishing takes you away from the distractions of everyday life and puts you in touch with your children. There are no TVs or telephones to interfere while you are fishing. This quiet time creates the perfect environment for listening and talking.

You say you don't know how to fish or don't know much about fishing! Don't be ashamed to admit that to yourself or to your children. Learning together will help make you and your family a better group of anglers, and at the same time help your children to build self-esteem, self-confidence and self-respect. Taking time for fun can be a positive alternative to drugs.

Please join us in helping our youth enjoy a drug-free environment while enjoying fishing as a lifelong form of recreation and entertainment.

ACKNOWLEDGEMENTS

Many people can take credit for the development of this Sport Fishing Aquatic Resources Education Student Manual, Intermediate Edition, for it truly was a team effort. The initial step was taken by the Aquatic Resource Education Council who provided support for the development of aquatic resource education programs by developing the *Aquatic Resources Education Curriculum,* a manual for teachers , in 1987. Without this momentous preliminary step, supported by the AFTMA Sport Fishing Educational Foundation, the development of this student manual might not have happened.

Both the author, Bob Schmidt, and the graphic artist, John Rice, have produced outstanding work to ensure the highest quality student materials available for aquatic resources education.

The experience, support, and suggestions of aquatic education professionals from thirteen states and the U.S. Fish and Wildlife Service had notable impact in shaping the content, scope, and sequence of this student manual. George Babey's exceptional dedication is acknowledged for his extensive review of the technical aquatic education segments of the text. In addition, gratitude is extended to the following group of professionals who critically reviewed the entire text:

Arkansas Game and Fish Commission—Sloan Lessley

Connecticut Department of Environmental Protection, Bureau of Fisheries—George Babey

Minnesota Division of Fish and Wildlife—Linda Erickson-Eastwood, Ilo Howard, and Roger Grosslein

Minnesota Division of Parks and Recreation—Judy Thomson

North Carolina Wildlife Commission—Kim Garner

New Mexico Game and Fish Department—Dan Shaw and Don MacCarter

Ohio Division of Wildlife—James R. Wentz, Steve Gray, Ken Fritz, Dave Ross and Jim Schoby

Oklahoma Department of Wildlife Conservation—Richard Fuller

Oregon Department of Fish and Wildlife—Bill Hastie

Pennsylvania Fish Commission—Stephen B. Ulsh

Virginia Department of Game & Inland Fisheries—Ann Skalski

Washington Department of Wildlife—Michael O'Malley

Wisconsin Department of Natural Resources—Tammy Peterson

U.S. Fish and Wildlife Service—Gary Edwards, Chuck Dunn, Steve Taub and Dave McDaniels

In addition the following associations and individuals assisted in the review and development of specific sections of the manual:

American Fisheries Society—Paul Brouha

Bureau of Land Management—Jack Williams

United States Coast Guard—Hunt Anderson

Izaak Walton League of America—David Dickson

Sport Fishing Institute—Norville Prosser

A cadre of exceptional teachers developed student activities which will be of interest to students of all ages, especially to those in the middle grades and junior high school:

Sidney W. Burnett, Shinnston, WV

Rudolph J. Cassetti, Jr., Shelton, CT

Judy Elsey, Terre Haute, IN

Frank Kucharski, Chester, CT

Ricky R. Murray, Clarksburg, WV

Richard E. Pratt, III, Nutter Fort, WV

Ben Wernz, Terre Haute, IN

A special thanks is extended to Sharon Rushton, Director of Education for the American Fishing Tackle Manufacturers Association, for her untiring efforts in communicating with, between, and among the state aquatic education and association professionals and the editor. Her labors have greatly enhanced the quality of the text.

This intermediate level Sport Fishing Aquatic Resources Education Student Manual was made possible through the American Fishing Tackle Manufacturers Association (AFTMA) Sport Fishing Educational Foundation. The Association's leadership is to be commended for its farsightedness and concern for the long-term advancement of aquatic resources by sponsoring the development of aquatic resources educational programs.

Louis R. Jensen
Indiana State University

Fishing. . . an Introduction

WHAT IS FISHING?

Fishing is trying to catch fish. It is one of the oldest and most popular outdoor activities.

The earliest evidence of primitive people shows that they fished using their bare hands and clubs. They used fish as food.

Throughout the years, new techniques were invented. Primitive people made spears out of bone, antler, horn, or stone. Often they would build a dam or a stream with rocks. The dam made a pool where the fish would gather, helping the fishermen catch fish.

Hooks have been used for fishing for thousands of years. The first hooks were made of animal bones, shells, bronze, antlers, and horns. The shape of hooks used by primitive people are very similar to those used today.

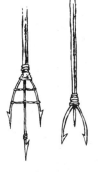

Today, more than 50 million people fish for recreational enjoyment. They are called anglers. Although the catch is often shared and eaten with other people, anglers **do not sell their catch.** Many anglers choose to practice catch and release fishing, returning their catch unharmed as soon as it is caught.

Sport fishing means different things to different people. Fishing

1

lets some people get away from the hustle and bustle of the daily routine to enjoy our nation's rich natural resources. Some people see fishing as an exciting and demanding sport. Others combine fishing with boating, picnicking, camping, backpacking and viewing wildlife.

Fishing is something everybody can do—boys, girls, moms, dads, grandparents. Even if someone has a disability, fishing offers a good time.

WHAT ARE AQUATIC RESOURCES?

Aquatic resources refer to things living in or on the water. This book is about aquatic resources education because it talks about more than just fish and fishing. In order to become a good angler, you need to know about where a fish lives—its **habitat**, water. Water is our greatest aquatic resource.

You'll also be introduced to many types of fish and places because what you do to the water in your state can impact fishing in another state or several states. Secondly, in your lifetime, you might have a chance to travel to other states. This book will also help you become familiar with fish and fishing techniques that you may not see in your home state.

2

CHAPTER
1
Let's Catch Fish

Fishing tackle is used to get your bait or lure to the fish. You don't need a lot of equipment to begin fishing. In fact, it's a good idea to begin with basic, simple tackle. You can try more difficult tackle after you've mastered some basic skills.

TYPES OF FISHING TACKLE

Pole and Line

The simplest fishing tackle is a pole; however, for some types of fishing, even a soda can with fishing line wrapped around it can be used!

The pole can be made of cane, bamboo or a straight piece of tree branch. You do not use a reel with a pole. Cut a piece of fishing line as long as the pole. Tie the line to the tip of the pole and a hook to the other end of the line. A small sinker, called a "split shot," is squeezed onto the line above the hook. The sinker makes it easier to swing the bait out into the water and keeps the bait under the surface. You may also want to use a bobber or float. By moving the bobber up or down the line, you can change the depth of your bait in the water. With a pole and line you can fish the area near the bank, where many fish often live.

Rods and Reels

Other types of fishing tackle use reels to store large amounts of line. They let you cast a bait or lure farther. They also help you retrieve lures correctly, fish in deeper water, and battle larger fish more easily. There are four kinds of reels: spincast, spinning, baitcast, and fly. Each kind uses a different type of rod.

Spincasting

Spincasting tackle is ideal for beginning anglers because it works well and is easy to use. A spincasting rod has small line guides and a straight handle. Spincasting tackle is often used while fishing for bluegill, crappie and other panfish. The spincasting reel mounts on top of the rod's handle. The fishing line comes out of a small hole in a cover on the front of the reel.

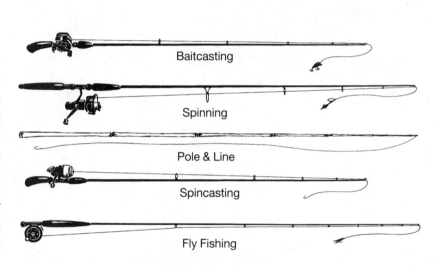

Baitcasting

Spinning

Pole & Line

Spincasting

Fly Fishing

Casting With a Spincasting

Outfit. To cast, grip the pistol grip with one hand. If you're right-handed, turn the rod sideways so the reel handle points straight up; if you're lefthanded, point the reel handle straight down. Push the reel's thumb button down and hold it down.

Face your target area and turn your body at a slight angle. The arm holding the rod should be closest to your target. Aim the rod tip toward the target-about level with your eyes.

Swiftly and smoothly, bend your casting arm at the elbow, raising your casting forearm until your hands reach eye level. When the rod is almost straight up, it will be bent back by the weight of the practice plug. As the rod bends, move your forearm forward with just a slight wrist movement. When the rod reaches eye level,

release the thumb button and let the line travel freely.

If the plug lands close in front of you, you released the thumb button too late. If the plug

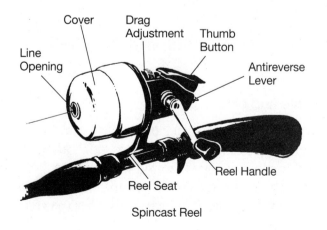

Cover

Drag Adjustment

Thumb Button

Line Opening

Antireverse Lever

Reel Seat

Reel Handle

Spincast Reel

4

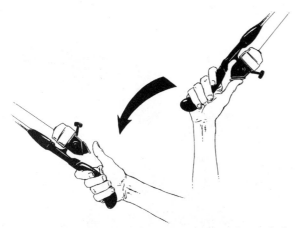

went more or less straight up, you released the button too soon.

Learning how to use a spincasting rod and reel isn't too hard, but it does take practice. Buy a practice casting plug. This is a rubber or plastic weight without hooks. Then, tie it to the end of the line. Find a spot where you can practice safely. Put a target on the ground about 25 feet away. Practice casting until you can consistently hit the target with your casting plug. Being able to hit a target is much more important than being able to cast a long distance!

Spinning

Spinning rods have a straight handle with large line guides that are on the bottom of the rod. A spinning reel is often called an "open-face" reel because the spool of fishing line isn't covered. The reel mounts under the handle. Spinning rods and reels allow for more line to be quickly peeled off the reel, allowing for casting longer distances.

Learning how to use a spinning outfit may take more practice than spincasting. Casting with a spinning outfit is very similar to using spincasting equipment. However, at the beginning you grasp the spinning rod's handle, placing the reel "stem" between your second and third fingers. Your thumb should be on top of the handle and your forefinger extended to touch the spool cover. With your other hand, rotate the reel spool until the line roller is directly beneath your extended forefinger. Pick up the line in front of the roller with your forefinger and open, or cock, the reel's bail with your other hand.

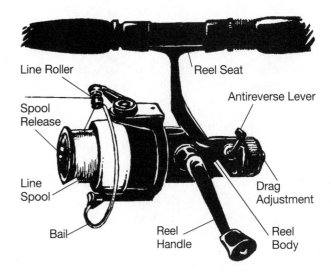

Spinning Reel

(Some reels have a lever so you can grasp the line and open the bail in one motion.)

After you have accomplished this procedure, casting is very similar to that for spincasting except that when the rod reaches your eye level as you are casting, you release the line from your forefinger rather than releasing the thumb botton. Again, if the plug lands close in front of you, your forefinger released the line too late. If the plug went more or less straight up, you released your forefinger too soon.

To prepare for practice follow the same steps as for spincasting.

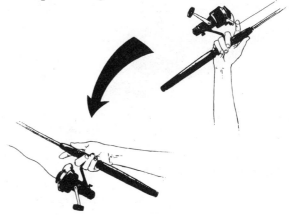

Baitcasting

A baitcasting rod can have either a pistol-type grip or a straight handle. As in spincasting, the casting reel and line guides are mounted on top of the rod. Unlike the other two types of reels, the casting reel's line spool turns as you cast and can

5

snarl the line if it is not controlled properly. Learning to control this spool makes casting tackle harder for most people to learn, and is considered a skill for advanced anglers.

Drag. All reels have an adjustment called a drag that controls how easily the line is pulled off the reel. When set correctly, the drag lets a larger fish pull some line from the reel until the fish becomes tired. Follow the directions that come with your reel to set the drag correctly.

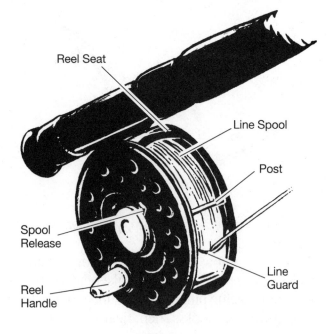

Fly Casting Reel

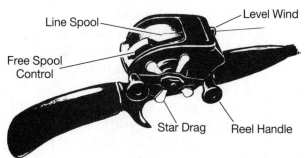

Baitcasting Reel

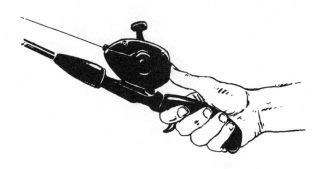

Flyfishing

Flyfishing tackle is different from all of the other types. In flyfishing, you are casting the line that carries the "fly." With other fishing tackle the weight of a bait or lure pulls line from a reel. In flyfishing, the reel is only used to store the line. Flycasting is usually the most difficult to learn. However, with proper instruction, anyone can learn how.

Saltwater

Saltwater tackle requires special equipment because saltwater will corrode any aluminum, steel or iron parts. The metal parts of saltwater tackle usually are made of stainless steel or nickel chrome. Saltwater tackle ranges from the ultralight equipment used in inshore fishing to the extremely large and heavy tackle for deep sea fishing.

Ice Fishing

Ice fishing is a very specialized sport. One- to three-foot rods are most often used. Simple reels are used to hold the line. Ice fishing can also be done with tip-ups. Tip-ups fit over a hole in the ice. When a fish hits, it releases a lever. This causes a flag to tip up, alerting the angler.

OTHER FISHING TACKLE

Fish Hooks

Fish hooks come in a variety of sizes and styles. When you fish with natural or live bait, a package with an assortment of hooks ranging from sizes No. 6 through No. 10 is suitable. However, when you fish for catfish or bullheads, larger hooks are needed.

The barbs on the hooks can be bent down if you intend to release your catch. This will make your fishing more challenging and reduce fish mortality.

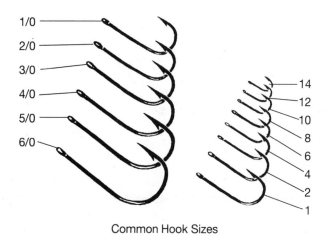

Common Hook Sizes

Fishing Line

Fishing line comes in a variety of sizes, or strengths, called **pound-test**. For example, ten pound-test line is stronger than four pound-test. You must match the pound-test line to the size of rod and reel, the bait you're using, and the fish you are fishing for. For example, small ultralight spincasting and spinning reels can use up to six-pound-test line. Larger spinning reels can use stronger line. Bait casting reels can use from 6- to 30-pound line, but 8- to 16-pound-test lines are most common. Using heavier line than necessary may reduce the number of bites or strikes you get, because heavy line is more visible in water.

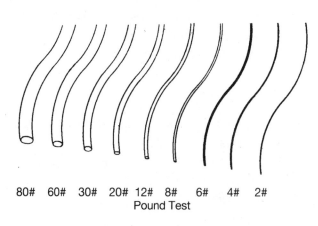

80# 60# 30# 20# 12# 8# 6# 4# 2#
Pound Test

To connect your line to your hook you need to learn to tie **fishing knots.** Although dozens of fishing knots are used you only need to learn two or three good knots for most fishing. Here's how to tie three common knots:

7

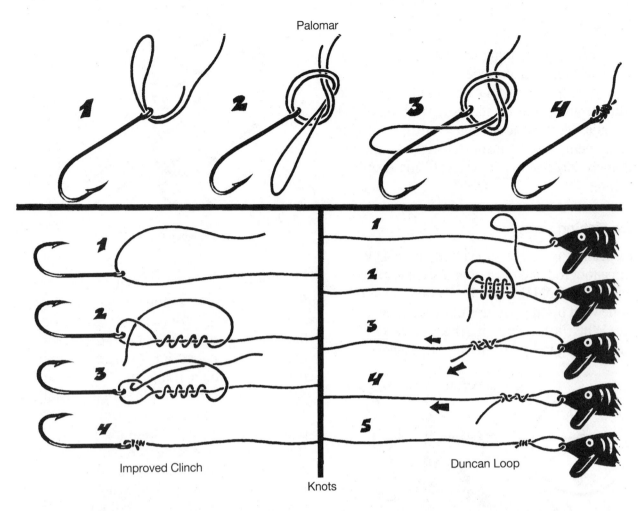

Palomar

1 2 3 4

Improved Clinch

1 2 3 4 5

Duncan Loop

Knots

The palomar and improved clinch knots are used by many anglers for attaching hooks and lures. They are both very strong knots.

The loop knot is used for minnow type baits and diving lures. The loop attached to the lure allows the lure to move more freely.

Sinkers

Sinkers range in size from split shot the size of a BB to weights of a pound or more. BB-size split shot to 1/4-ounce sinkers are most common. Sinkers allow you to cast your bait and help take it down to the bottom.

Bobbers

Bobbers are used to keep your bait at the depth you want it. They also help you to know when you have a strike. Use a bobber that's just large enough to keep your bait from dragging it under

the water. Pencil style bobbers are more sensitive than round ones. Because of this it is easier to tell if a fish is biting. Round bobbers are easier to cast. Slip bobbers can be easily adjusted to allow you to fish at different depths. Their main advantage is that they are easy to cast. They come in both round and pencil styles.

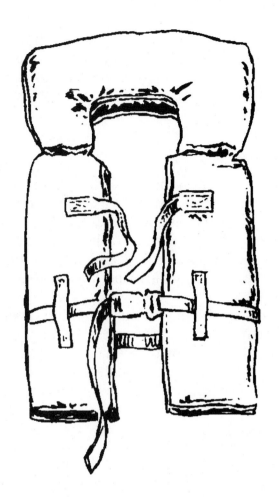

Many bobbers attach to fishing line with a spring clip and move up or down the line easily, depending on how deep you want to fish your bait.

Tackle Box

A tackle box is useful for storing hooks, sinkers, bobbers, lures, and other things you need for fishing. A small, top-opening box with two trays is a good first box.

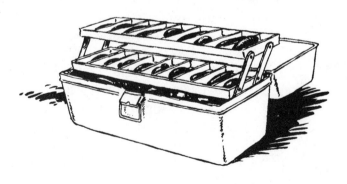

Personal Flotation Device (PFD)

A personal flotation device, also known as a life jacket, should be part of your essential fishing gear. You should always wear one if you are fishing near deep or fast moving water. When you are fishing from a boat, you must always wear a PFD. If you choose a PFD with pockets, you can also use it as a fishing vest to hold your tackle.

Other Accessories

Other equipment anglers find useful includes a container for live bait, snaps and swivels, a line clipper, long-nose pliers with wire cutters, a hook disgorger for removing fish hooks, a fish scaler, and a stringer or ice chest to keep your fish fresh. In addition, you should always have your first-aid kit with you.

NATURAL BAITS AND BAITING YOUR HOOK

As you learn more about fish behavior you'll learn more about how to choose the best bait for different situations. Several types of live or natural bait will help you catch fish. Always check your fishing regulations to make sure the bait you choose is legal for the lake you are fishing.

Some of the best baits for freshwater fishing include worms, leeches, minnows, crayfish, crickets and grasshoppers. Good saltwater baits include sea worms, eels, crabs, shrimp, strips of squid, and cut-up pieces of fish.

Worms

Worms are a good bait for nearly all freshwater and saltwater fish, although sea worms are often used in saltwater fishing. You can find enough worms for fishing from a few shovels of dirt in your garden or from a shaded, damp area. Worms can also be purchased in fishing tackle stores and bait shops.

If you have small worms, thread the hook through the side of the worm at several places along its body. For bait-stealing fish such as sunfish, thread the worm on the hook until the hook is completely covered.

Minnows

Minnows must be stored in a minnow bucket with plenty of cool water to keep them alive. Never crowd them.

One way to hook a minnow is through both lips, beginning with the bottom lip. You can also hook a minnow through the tail, behind the head, or through the back.

Crickets and Grasshoppers

Both land and water insects can be used for bait. When using small insects, you should use hooks made of thin wire.

Bait Leeches

Leeches are excellent bait for many fish. They should be hooked through the sucker in the tail.

Clams, Mussels, and Sea Worms

These baits are good for perch, drum, sea trout, and rockfish. Completely remove their shell and thread onto the hook.

Shrimp

Shrimp can be used either alive or dead for saltwater fish. Hook the shrimp through the tail. You can also peel off the shell and thread cut up pieces of shrimp on the hook.

PREPARED BAITS

For bottom-feeding fish like carp and catfish, bread, small pieces of cheese, and canned corn are good. You can buy commercially made baits. Many anglers, however, like to make their own bait for these fish. Here are two recipes for bait to catch bottom-feeding fish:

Carp Doughballs

1. Mix 1 cup of flour, 1 cup of yellow cornmeal, and 1 teaspoon of sugar in a bowl.
2. Take a 1-quart container of water and pour just enough of it into the mixture to make a heavy dough.
3. Roll the dough into balls about 1/2 inch to 1 inch in diameter.
4. Mix the rest of the water with 1 cup of molasses and pour it into a pan.
5. Put the pan on the stove and bring the molasses and water to a boil.

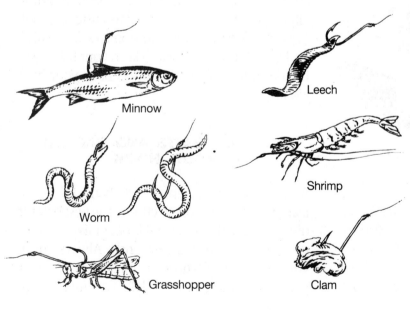

Minnow

Leech

Worm

Shrimp

Grasshopper

Clam

6. When the mixture is boiling, drop in several doughballs, but don't overcrowd them. Cook them for 2 to 3 minutes.
7. Cook the rest of the doughballs, a few at a time, in the same way.

You can store the cooked doughballs in the leftover water and molasses.

When using doughballs or stinkbait (a smelly catfish bait) use small treble hooks. A treble hook has three points. Some have a spring wrapped around the shank to help hold the bait.

Many manufacturers make a variety of "stinkbaits." Homemade stinkbait can be made using the following recipe.

Catfish Stinkbait

1. Fill a jar with pieces of a forage fish like shad.
2. Cover the jar with the lid, but leave the lid loose so gases will escape.
3. Put the jar in direct sunlight for a day or two.

When you open the jar, you'll know your catfish "stinkbait" is ready to use.

LURES

Fishing lure companies make lures in many sizes, styles, colors, and patterns. Read the instructions in or on a lure package to learn how to use each lure. Here are a few types of lures:

Jigs

Jigs have weighted metal heads and a "tail" made

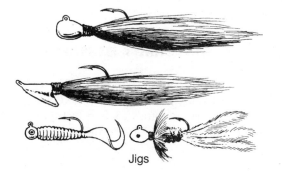

Jigs

of animal hair, soft plastic, feathers, or rubber. Anglers sometimes add a minnow or piece of pork rind to the jig's hook. Jigs can be used to catch nearly every kind of freshwater and many saltwater fish.

Spoons

Spoons are metal lures designed to look like a swimming baitfish. Many spoons are made to be cast. Others are meant to be trolled behind a moving boat.

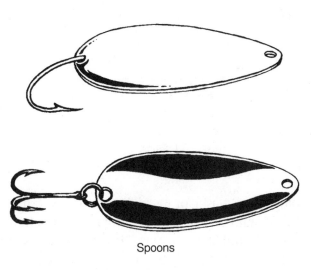

Spoons

Plastic Baits

Soft-plastic worms, minnows, and crayfish are available in many sizes and colors. You can use them with or without a weight. Sometimes,

Plastic Baits

11

plastic baits are used with a jig head, spinner or spinnerbait. Some plastic baits have scents attractive to fish built into them.

Plugs

Plugs have a body made of plastic or wood and are designed to be used on top of the water or at depths below the surface. Topwater or floating plugs are designed to float on the surface. Diving

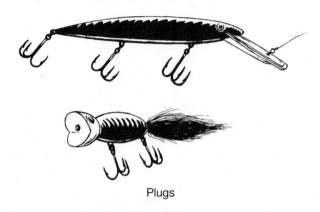
Plugs

plugs have plastic or metal lips so they will dive to a certain depth. These diving plugs are often called "crankbaits" because they are often used with baitcasting reels that operate like a crank.

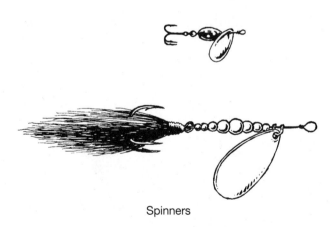
Spinners

Spinners

Spinners have one or more blades that spin, or revolve, around a straight wire shaft. Some spinners have tails made of soft plastic or animal hair.

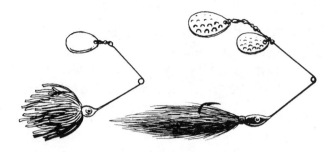
Spinnerbaits

Spinnerbaits

Spinnerbaits are lures with one or more blades that spin around a "safety pin"-type shaft. Most spinnerbaits have skirts made from animal hair, vinyl, rubber, or other materials.

Poppers and Flies

Poppers and Flies

Poppers and flies are small lures used with spincast and flyfishing tackle. These baits are very good for panfish and other fish that feed on the surface such as trout and bass. Fly tying can be a very rewarding hobby.

As you understand more about the environment fish live in and how they behave, you will learn which bait or lure is best for specific fish during different seasons of the year.

ACTIVITIES

ACTIVITY 1 — VISITING A FISHING TACKLE STORE
After reading this chapter, take your book to your local fishing tackle store. Locate the items of equipment mentioned to see how they look in real life. Ask the owner to show you the different types of lures, rods and

reels, fish hooks, and fishing lines, commercially prepared baits, and other equipment. Have him explain anything that you do not understand.

ACTIVITY 2 — KNOT TYING

Find a piece of heavy twine or thin clothesline and a bolt with a big eye to represent the hole in a hook. Practice tying the palomar, improved clinch, and loop knots described in your book. Practice until you can tie these knots without looking at the directions. Practice with monofilament line after you have learned how to tie these knots.

ACTIVITY 3 — PRACTICE CASTING

Place a piece of cardboard in your yard, driveway, or other safe place. Take your fishing outfit with a practice plug without hooks. Stand about 25 feet away and practice your casting by aiming at your cardboard target.

Practice until you can hit your target regularly. To make a game of this, make three targets and with two friends have a casting contest. Each person gets 10 casts. Count three points for each cast that hits the target and one point for a plug that hits the ground and bounces onto the target. The highest score wins.

ACTIVITY 4 — COLLECTING YOUR OWN BAIT

Look on your lawn at night after a rain. Cover the lens of a flashlight with red cellophane so that the light won't scare the worms back into the ground. When you see one, grasp it quickly just below the collar-the enlarged part of the worm's body. Don't try to pull it out at once. As soon as you grasp it, the worm will try to crawl back into its burrow. Just hold on for a few seconds until the worm relaxes and can be removed easily.

Fishing Safely

Fishing isn't a dangerous sport, but you should prepare to keep safe and comfortable in the outdoors. It is possible to get caught unexpectedly in bad weather, encounter insects, spend too much time in the sun, or get caught on a fish hook.

Wearing the proper clothing helps to protect you from injury. It also keeps you warm in cold weather and cool in hot weather. Rainwear and other gear keep you from getting wet and chilled.

Avoid problems by preparing for the unexpected.

SAFETY AROUND WATER

Water accidents claim many lives each year. Obviously you will be around water if you are fishing and accidents can happen at any moment, sending you into the water. A bank can give way if you are careless onshore. You can slip on a rock, step into a deep hole while wading, or fall out of a boat.

Anglers should **learn how to swim and use caution around water at all times.** You should always use the "buddy system" and have a friend or an adult with you in case something goes wrong.

Types of PFDs

Personal Flotation Devices (PFDs)

Personal Flotation Devices (PFDs), often called "life vests," are not just for wearing in boats. Anytime you are on or around deep or fast-moving water, **it is always best to be wearing your PFD.** U.S. Coast Guard and/or state laws require you to have an approved PFD when you are in a boat. The rules say a boat must have one PFD for each person on board. Certain types of boats must also have a cushion or ring that can be thrown to a person in the water.

Wading

There are several rules you should follow for safe wading.

---

1. Always wade with another person.
2. Always wear your PFD.
3. Find out how deep the water is.
4. Find out how strong the current is.
5. Find out what the bottom is like.
6. Use a stick or staff. Shuffle your feet along the bottom to avoid holes.

While wading you can protect your ankles by wearing high-top shoes or wading boots. Long, lightweight pants can protect you from jellyfish and sea nettles in saltwater and from snags and rocks in freshwater.

Reach-Throw-Row-Go

Reach-throw-row-go is a method of rescuing a person who falls overboard or an angler or swimmer in trouble.

The first safety step is to **REACH out with an oar, tree limb, or other long object if the person is close to you.** If you can't reach the person, then **THROW them a life-saving device.** This can be a boat cushion or ring that floats. If possible, it should be tied to the end of a line so you can pull the person to you. If a cushion or ring isn't handy, anything that floats can be thrown. Plastic coolers, ski belts, or even beach balls can be used in an emergency.

If there is nothing to throw, **ROW a boat to the person in trouble.** There should be someone else in the boat to help pull the person in trouble into the boat. The person should be pulled in over the stern, or back, of the boat. If the boat has a motor, it must be shut off before you get to the person in the water. Don't let the person try to climb in over the side of a small boat. This can tip the boat over. If the boat is small, have the victim hang on the gunwales, and tow him to shore.

Swim out to save the person in trouble **ONLY** as a last resort and **ONLY** if you are an experienced lifeguard or have had life-saving training. **GOing** into the water after the person in trouble is very dangerous. People who are drowning often panic and injure or even drown someone trying to rescue them. **GOing** quickly for help is often the best choice.

Swimming

If you fish, you should know how to swim for your own safety. Many young anglers like to go for a swim during a fishing trip just for fun or to cool off. Don't swim if there is any doubt about your ability. Never dive into the water of an unknown area and don't swim after a heavy meal or in cold water. Swim only when an experienced swimming partner is with you.

Safety With Fishing Equipment

Handle your fishing equipment responsibly. Hooks can be dangerous if you do not handle them properly. Look behind you before you cast to make sure your hook will not be caught on a power line, a tree, or a person. If you leave your

Reach

Throw

Row

Go

sleeved shirts. In warm weather lightweight and light-colored clothing reflects the sun and is cooler. Dark clothing is warmer because it absorbs heat.

Even in warm weather it's a good idea to take a sweater or jacket and rain gear. Even though it may be warm during much of the day, many fishing trips begin early when it's still chilly and end late in the evening when it gets cool.

Western-style hats offer good protection from glare and against sunburn. Lightweight, light-colored, baseball-style caps are also popular and will help keep you cooler. In tropical areas, such as Florida and the Gulf Coast, some saltwater anglers put a cloth on the back of their caps to keep their necks from getting sunburned. Hats also protect your head from hooks on poor casts.

A pair of high-top sneakers is ideal for protecting your feet from sharp rocks and glass while wading in the summer. They will also protect your feet while you are fishing from the bank. For fishing from a boat wear shoes designed to keep you from slipping on a wet boat deck (boat shoes).

tackle laying on the ground, another person can trip on it and fall, step on a hook, or break your tackle.

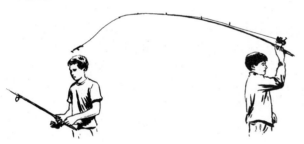

Look Before Casting

Take caution and use long-nose pliers to help remove hooks from a fish. If a hook is deep inside the fish, either cut off the line and leave the hook in the fish, or use a hook disgorger. Hooks left in fish will work themselves free or rust out.

When transporting your equipment, remove the hook or lure from your line and store it in your tackle box.

FISHING IN WARM WEATHER

Because the hot summer sun is harmful your skin must be protected as much as possible when fishing. Long pants and long shirt sleeves provide better protection than shorts and short-

16

FISHING IN COLD WEATHER

If you fish in cold weather, several layers of clothing can keep you warm. Clothing layers trap air between them and offer great insulation. As it warms up during the day, you can always take off some of the clothing.

Long underwear, a warm shirt, and warm pants help to hold your body's heat. Additional layers of clothing can include an insulated vest and a rain parka, which are also good for keeping you warm on cold, windy days.

Caps and hats are important. They prevent loss of body heat from your head-and-neck area. Headgear used for fishing during the winter should protect most of your head, including your ears. Some good choices are an insulated hat or cap or a wool stocking cap. A knit scarf can protect your neck.

Fishing is difficult with most gloves. There are gloves, however, that let you tie knots and handle fishing tackle. They include lightweight rubber gloves and "hunter/fisherman's gloves," gloves that have a flap so you can expose your fingers. Gloves without fingertips are also good.

Before fishing on ice, it is a good safety practice to check the thickness of the ice. Drill a hole with an ice auger near shore and along your route of travel, measuring the thickness of the ice as you move. Do not fish on ice unless it is at least four inches, and preferably more, thick. Thinner ice is dangerous because it can break easily.

You need warm clothing, long underwear, pants and shirt for cold weather and ice fishing.

A snowmobile suit and insulated boots with thick soles are ideal. A warm hat, heavy gloves, and a skier's mask are also needed. Hand warmers are also helpful. A personal flotation device, when worn under clothing, provides extra warmth and also emergency flotation if you go for an unexpected icy plunge.

GENERAL PROTECTION ITEMS NEEDED FOR ALL-WEATHER FISHING

Sunscreens

Anglers should avoid suntanning, which is harmful to the skin. We get vitamin D from the sun, so it can be helpful. However, too much sun can cause skin cancer. A sunscreen lotion can and should be used to keep the sun's ultraviolet (UV) rays from reaching your skin. One with a Sun Protection Factor (SPF) of 15 on the label gives good protection.

Rainwear

All anglers must have rainwear. Several styles are available. A rain poncho is good, but many anglers prefer a two-piece rain suit with a jacket and pants.

Good rainwear is waterproof, not just water-repellant. It should have a full hood to protect your head, a storm flap over the jacket opening, a zipper, buttons or snaps, and elastic around the cuff and ankle openings to keep water out.

Sunglasses

Sunglasses protect your eyes against the sun's glare from the water. Many anglers like polarized sunglasses that reduce glare and let them see below the surface of the water to spot fish and other objects. Some sunglasses are treated to protect your eyes from the sun's harmful ultraviolet light rays.

Hip Boots and Waders

Hip boots and waders are designed to keep you dry and protect you against the chill of cool water. For cold-water wading, wear insulated boots. Hip boots only come up to your hips and are held in place with belt straps. Waders come up to the top part of your chest. They are held in place by suspenders and you should wear a belt on the outside. They will protect you while surf fishing, wading a stream, or fishing in deeper water.

Under most circumstances, if you fall in the water with your hip-boots on, do not try to remove them; first bend your knees. Air trapped in the boots will make them float at the toes. This can help keep you afloat as you paddle toward shore.

INSECTS AND INSECT BITES

Insects can be pests. Common ones are mosquitoes, chiggers, ticks, black flies, bees, wasps, and hornets. While you cannot avoid insects entirely, there are some things you can do.

1. Try to avoid areas with lots of insects.
2. Don't use cologne, perfume, or other scents that might attract them.
3. Don't wear blue clothing. Blue seems to attract mosquitoes.
4. Wear a long-sleeved shirt and long pants.
5. Turn up your shirt collar.
6. Use an insect repellent, but do not get it on your lures or bait since fish can smell it and may not bite.

No one likes sunburn and insect bites, but they happen. Aloe vera and other salves and lotions can provide relief for minor cases of sunburn. Insect bites and stings can be dangerous. If you have extreme reactions to a sting, carry a special prescription injection kit for such an emergency.

For most people, removing the bee's stinger and applying a pain-killing balm or a paste of baking soda or meat tenderizer will help to relieve the pain and reduce swelling, itching, and inflammation. Remember to always scrape a bee

stinger from your skin. Squeezing it and pulling can inject more poison and prolong your discomfort.

BASIC FIRST AID

Removing a Hook From Your Skin

Occasionally an angler will get a fish hook in the skin. Removing a fish hook is best left to a doctor or a hospital's emergency room. Once a fish hook enters the skin beyond the barb, it is hard to remove. *Never* remove a hook from around a person's eyes, face, the back of the hands, or any area where ligaments, tendons, or blood vessels are visible.

There is a method that can be used to remove a hook if it is not in a vital area. First cut the hook away from the rest of the fishing lure. Then, put a loop of heavy twine or fishing line around the bend of the hook. Next, hold down the eye and shank of the hook, pressing it lightly to the skin. Grasp the loop in the line and, with a sharp jerk, pull the hook free.

Any hook wound should be followed by a tetanus shot if the victim has not had one in the past five years.

Cuts and Bleeding

In all cases of serious bleeding where there is a large or deep cut, call a doctor, get the victim to a hospital, or call paramedics at once. Small cuts can be handled by adhesive bandages and antiseptic. For large or deep cuts, pressing directly on the wound with a clean gauze pad or handkerchief will reduce bleeding. Use the procedure taught at Red Cross training courses to ensure that proper amounts of pressure are applied.

Hypothermia

Hypothermia means your body is losing heat faster that it can produce it. Without treatment your life is in danger. Exposure to the cold along with wind, wetness and exhaustion causes hypothermia. It doesn't have to be freezing cold for

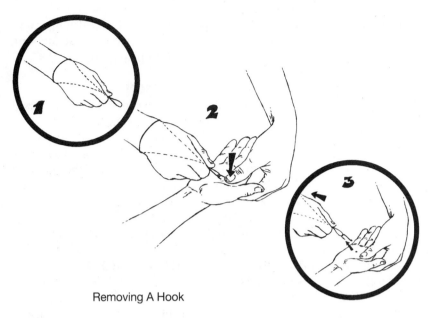

Removing A Hook

up heat loss. Instead, bring your knees up towards your chin and bend your legs as though you are sitting. This is called the Heat Escape Lessening Position or "H.E.L.P." This helps hold body heat and slows cooling.

To detect hypothermia, watch for these signs: uncontrollable shivering, fumbling hands, frequent stumbling, a lurching walk, vague slow speech, drowsiness or apparent exhaustion.

To treat hypothermia, get the victim out of the cold. Give warm drinks, remove all wet clothing and get the victim into dry clothes, and if possible, into a warm sleeping bag next to another person to provide body heat. Try to keep the person awake.

Other Medical Problems

Snake bites and broken bones are rare, but serious, emergencies. A person with a broken bone should not be moved until medical help is found.

Snakes rarely bite if they are left alone. A person bitten by a poisonous snake should be kept calm and quiet and taken to a doctor or hospital at once. If possible, determine the type of snake that caused the bite.

you to develop hypothermia. Many cases of hypothermia develop in air temperatures between 30 and 50 degrees F. Cold water takes away body heat 25 times faster than air of the same temperature. Any water colder than 70 degrees can cause hypothermia.

H. E. L. P. Position

To protect yourself from hypothermia stay warm and dry. Remember that wind makes you colder. If you fall into cold water with a PFD on, don't thrash around. Excess movement speeds

ACTIVITIES

ACTIVITY 1 — FISHING SAFETY-SELF TEST
For each given situation below, think of a possible accident and a safety practice to avoid this accident.
1. Wading in streams
2. Fishing from a bank
3. Fishing from rocks
4. Fishing from boats
5. Fishing from piers
6. Fishing from a boat in rough water
7. Ice fishing
8. Wearing waders/ hip boots
9. Tangled messy tackle box
10. Fishing in a crowded area
11. Handling a hooked fish
12. Handling an unhooked fish

13. Climbing, leaning and reaching while in a boat
14. Fishing gear not properly secured
15. Fishing or boating without PFDs
16. Fishing or boating on a hot sunny day
17. Fishing or boating on a cold, wet day
18. Fishing or boating and using alcohol
19. Fishing without a buddy
20. Fishing/swimming in unfamiliar waters
21. Horseplay near the water
22. Fishing at night from boat or shore
23. Cleaning and/or filleting fish
24. Disobeying posted signs
25. Overloading a boat

ACTIVITY 2 — WHAT SHALL I WEAR?

Place sheets of different colored construction paper or scraps of fabric in the sun. After five minutes feel each one. Are the dark-colored ones warmer or cooler than the light colored ones? What does this tell you about the color of clothing to wear to stay cool while fishing during the summer? What color of clothing should you wear in the winter?

ACTIVITY 3 — WATCH THAT REFLECTION.

Place a small mirror in the sun. Angle it towards your hand or arm. Do you feel the intensity of the sun? If the sun is in the right position when you are fishing from a boat you get reflected sunlight that can cause sunburn, just like the reflected light from a mirror.

ACTIVITY 4 — INSULATION

Materials: insulated cup, paper cup (same size), covers of cardboard, 2 thermometers and water.

Heat enough water for both cups to 180 degrees F. Fill both cups to the same level. Poke a hole in the cover for each cup and insert the thermometers to the same depth in the water. Note the temperature in each cup every 3 minutes. Which cools faster?

The insulated cup holds more of the heat in. Would insulated clothing help keep you warm?

ACTIVITY 5 — PRACTICING HOOK REMOVAL

With your teacher or another adult and using the procedure described in this chapter, use an orange to practice hook removal.

ACTIVITY 6 — MAKING A FIRST-AID KIT

With an adult's assistance, make a list of things that should go into a basic-first aid kit to carry while you are fishing. Gather these items and make a first-aid kit to pack with your fishing gear.

3

Caring For Your Catch

Many fish are used as food. Fish are a good source of protein and are eaten by people around the world.

A fish that you plan to eat must be kept fresh. To ensure its freshness it must be kept alive until it is cleaned. You can put live fish in the livewell of a boat or on a stringer in the water. If a fish can't be kept alive, it should be cleaned and placed on ice to avoid spoilage. If you don't plan to keep a fish, free it quickly without harming it.

RELEASING A FISH

To release a fish, keep it in the water if you can. Handle it carefully with a wet hand so it can be freed unharmed. If it's a fish without sharp teeth like a bass, hold its lower lip between your thumb and index finger. If it has sharp teeth like a walleye or northern pike, carefully hold it around the body. Never hold a fish by the eyes or gills if it will be released.

Never tear a hook out. This can harm the fish and it may not live. If the fish is hooked deeply and you can't easily remove the hook, cut the line to release the fish. The hook will rust, dissolve, or become loose without harming the fish.

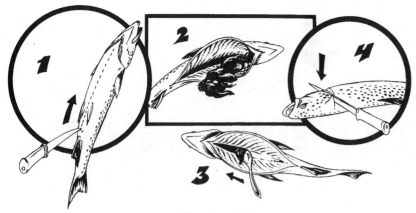

Cleaning a Fish

the scales from the tail toward the head with a fish scaler or a large spoon. Remove the scales on both sides of the body. After you remove the head, gills, guts, and fins, cook the fish with its skin on.

Small fish, like bluegill and crappie, are usually scaled, cleaned and then cooked whole. Cook scaled fish with the bones in the body and remove them just before you eat.

If a fish loses consciousness, try to revive it by gently moving it forward and backward so water moves through its gills. When the fish begins to struggle and can swim, let it go.

CLEANING FISH TO EAT

Ask an adult to teach you how to use a knife to dress a fish so nobody gets hurt.

First insert the knife tip into the fish's vent and move the blade up along the belly, cutting to the head. Keep the knife blade shallow so you don't puncture the intestines. Then, spread the body open and remove all of the entrails. Some fish have a kidney by the backbone. You can remove it by scraping it out with a spoon or your thumbnail. Cut off the head and rinse the fish in clean water.

To keep a dressed fish fresh, surround it with ice in an ice chest or cooler. As the ice melts it should drain from the cooler. Never store fish in ice water.

Most saltwater fish don't keep well when put in a livewell or kept on a stringer. They must be put on ice to keep them fresh.

Scaling

Scaling means to remove the scales from the skin of a fish. Scale fish on a flat surface using one hand to hold it by the head. Rake

Scaling a Fish

Skinning

Removing the skin improves the taste of many fish. It also removes a layer of fat just under the skin. Catfish are usually skinned.

To skin a catfish or bullhead, hold its head firmly on a flat surface with a clamp. For safety,

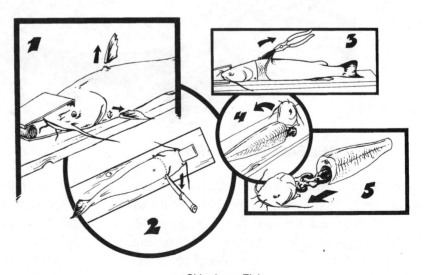

Skinning a Fish

22

it is a good idea to snip off a catfish's spines before skinning. Then, cut through the skin behind the head and the pectoral fins. Use pliers to remove the skin from the body, pulling from the head toward the tail. Grasp the head of the fish with one hand and the body with the other. Break the backbone at the head. Pull

Filleting a Fish

the head and guts away from the skinned body. After you wash the fish in clean water, it's ready for cooking. You remove the fish's bones just before you eat it.

People also fillet catfish. However, they are more difficult to fillet than most other fish.

Filleting

Filleting means getting the meat of the fish without the bones. Larger fish, such as largemouth bass, northern pike, salmon, and walleye, are usually filleted. A filleted fish has its skin and all of its bones removed before cooking. Scaling isn't necessary. Fillet knives have a long, thin, blade that's very sharp and specifically designed for filleting fish.

Have an adult help as you learn to fillet. A fillet knife is dangerous and must be handled safely. If you have any slime on your hands or the knife handle, wash it off to prevent slipping. Always keep your hands in back of the blade. For added safety, wear metal-mesh "fish-cleaning" gloves to protect your hands.

To fillet a fish, lay it on its side on a flat surface. Cut the fish behind its gills and pectoral fin down to, but not through, the backbone. Without removing the knife, turn the blade and cut through the ribs toward the tail. Use the fish's backbone to guide you. Turn the fish over and repeat the steps.

Next, insert the knife blade close to the rib bones and slice the entire rib section of each fillet away. Then, with the skin side down, insert the knife blade about a 1/2 inch from the tail. Gripping this tail part firmly, put the blade between the skin and the meat at an angle. Using a little

pressure and a sawing motion, cut against—not through—the skin. The fillet will be removed from the skin.

Wash each fillet in cold water. Pat dry with a clean cloth or paper towel. The fillets are ready to cook or freeze.

Steaking

A large fish is often cut across the body into thick steaks. First, clean the fish and skin or scale it. Usually, a fish is scaled only if the scales make it difficult to cut the steaks. Before steaking, chill the fish or put it in a freezer until it is partly stiff.

For most fish, cut through the body, working from the tail toward the head. Make each steak from 1/2-inch to 1-inch thick. After steaking, trim away any belly fat or bones that you can see, but not the backbone.

STORING FISH

Keep a fish alive or chilled from the time it is caught until it can be stored. Clean it as soon as possible to preserve its flavor. However, a fish can be kept for up to a day before cleaning if it is iced or chilled. After a fish is cleaned and skinned, filleted, or steaked, there are several ways to store it.

Icing

After a fish is dressed you can ice it. This is the best way to transport fish. Use an insulated cooler and leave the cooler's drain plug open so ice water will run out. Water spoils the flavor of the fish.

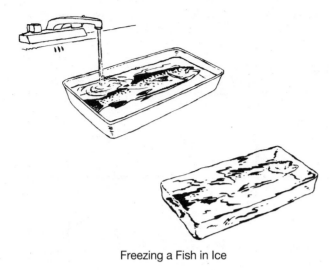

Freezing a Fish in Ice

Refrigeration

Before refrigerating a fish, wash it in cold water and dry it with a clean cloth or paper towel. Then wrap it in waxed paper, plastic wrap, or aluminum foil and store on ice in the refrigerator. Usually, you can store a fish in the refrigerator for up to two days. Large fish or large pieces of fish will keep longer than small pieces. Lean fish (panfish and walleye) store better than fatty fish (trout).

Freezing

Frozen fish last from three to twelve months. However, the preparation for freezing is important.

A fish can lose its flavor if it comes in contact with air. One way to prevent this is to wrap the fish in aluminum foil. Then, wrap it again with freezer paper.

Another way is to freeze the fish in a solid block of ice. Use a refrigerator container. Place the fish into the container, but use enough water to just cover the fish.

To thaw a frozen fish, put it in the refrigerator overnight or place the wrapped fish in cold water. Do not try to thaw fish in a microwave because part of the fish will begin to cook before other parts are thawed. Don't thaw fish at room temperature.

Other Ways

Smoking, pickling, and canning are other ways to store or prepare fish. Look for recipes in cookbooks or your public library.

WAYS TO COOK FISH

Frying

Many fish are panfried; however, broiling or baking are also popular methods of cooking fish. Panfrying is nothing more than cooking both sides of the fish in hot cooking oil. Coat the fish with flour, breading, cornmeal or batter before frying. The batter mix can be a pancake-type batter or one made with spices or even a little baking soda. Make sure the oil is hot enough. Heat the oil in a skillet and put a small piece of fish in it. If it sizzles, the oil is hot enough.

To deep-fry fish, put them completely into a deep pan of hot cooking oil. Fillets or small fish can be used with or without batter.

Recipes

There are many recipes for cooking fish. Most cookbooks have them. Here's a simple recipe for panfried fish.

Panfried Fish
   Ingredients:
   Lean whole fish, dressed
   1/2 cup milk
   1 egg
   1/2 cup flour
   Salt, pepper, and herb seasoning
   Cooking oil, butter, or margarine
   Lemon
   Parsley

Mix the egg and milk. Dip the fish into the egg-milk mixture and then coat the fish with flour. Instead of flour, you can use a heavier, breaded coating or pancake batter. Turn on the burner and set it to a high heat. Put some oil, butter, or margarine into the cooking pan. Use enough to cover the bottom to a depth of 1/8 to 1/4 inch. When the oil is hot enough, put in the fish. Adjust the heat so that the oil will not smoke or burn. Cook the fish until it is brown on one side. Then, turn it over and cook the other side until it's brown, too. Remove the fish from the pan and place it on a paper towel to drain. Put the fish on a serving platter and sprinkle with lemon juice and parsley. Butter and herbs are also tasty on panfried fish.

Other Ways To Cook Fish

There are many ways to cook fish that are both tasty and healthy. Broiling, grilling, baking, and poaching are good ways to cook fish. People prefer to fix fish these ways for a change and because oil is not used. This makes them healthier for those people who have to watch their diets. You can ask your parents if you can help as they prepare fish in these ways.

The microwave is an especially good way to cook fish quickly and easily. Place fillets in a microwave dish, add a liquid like water or lemon juice, cover them, and cook on high for six or seven minutes for one pound of fillets. Let stand for five minutes and then eat.

SAFETY OF EATING FISH

Most fish are safe to eat. However, some waters are polluted in such a way that it makes some fish unsafe to eat. Most often the health benefits of adding low-cholesterol fish to your diet greatly outweigh any health risks. If you are unsure of the safety of the area you are fishing, contact your state's natural resources agency or health department.

Some pollution problems in fish can be re-duced by cleaning fish carefully. Skinning fish removes fat under the skin. Many pollutants can be contained in this fat. Trim fat from around the backbone, along the sides, and from the belly of the fish.

ACTIVITIES

ACTIVITY 1 — CARE OF YOUR CATCH

With adult supervision, clean and prepare a fish you have caught. If you have more than one fish you can use different methods to prepare them for storing or cooking. Depending on the species you can scale, skin, or fillet your fish. If you do not plan to immediately eat the fish, prepare it for freezing following the procedure listed in this chapter. Perform all of the necessary steps yourself, realizing some assistance may be required.

ACTIVITY 2 — PREPARING FISH TO EAT

One of the best aspects of fishing is actually eating the fish. Before you even catch one of your own, you can try your hand at cooking.

Buy any type of fish fillet; even inexpensive fish are delicious if prepared properly. There are many ways to cook fish, but choose to fry, broil, or grill your fish fillets. After cooking the fish have your family sample your cooking.

ACTIVITY 3 — POND FOOD

Besides the fish you catch, there is another very tasty food that you can prepare from a pond. The common cattail grows in abundance in almost every pond.

In the spring of the year try this vegetable: In the shallow water, find cattail shoots sticking up about two feet. Pull gently and they should come loose below the water line. There will be a white section several inches long at the end. Cut this off and peel off the outer layers and boil in salted water for three to four minutes. Drain and top with some butter. This is "Cossack asparagus".

ACTIVITY 4 — RECIPE BOOK

Start a cookbook of fish recipes: include the favorites of your family and ask your friends for their family's favorites. Be sure to tell how to prepare the fish before cooking including the use of any seasoning or spices. Write each recipe on an index card in a card file for future reference. Recipes can be organized by species of fish and then by the type of cooking method.

CHAPTER
4
Fishing From Shore

Shore fishing offers many opportunities for anglers. You can fish from the banks of rivers and streams, the shorelines of inland lakes and ponds, and in the surf on the Atlantic, Pacific and Gulf coasts. You can also fish from manmade structures such as piers, jetties, walkways, and bridges.

Shore fishing is available to everyone, even large family and club groups. And because there's no boat to own or rent, it's low in cost.

FISHING LOCATIONS

Many anglers often fish from shore. Although some species of fish are rarely caught by shore anglers, there are still plenty of other species available to shore anglers. For example, free-swimming ocean fish are not found close to shore. Others like deep-dwelling lake trout are not often caught by shore anglers. Fish commonly caught by shore anglers include species that live near structure (bass, northern pike, sunfish, and stream trout) and those that feed on the bottom (carp, catfish, suckers, perch and walleye).

One big advantage of shore angling is that almost everyone has some body of water near home that offers fishing.

Shore Fishing

Lakes and Ponds

Many lakes and ponds have shoreline structure such as docks, logs, stump fields, brush and rock piles, and downed trees. Such things, which provide shelter, shade, and protection for fish, are ideal fishing spots. The best locations may be remote and far from roads.

Rivers and Streams

Rivers and streams are also good p especially those with structure such as islands, sand bars, rocks or rock piles, and log jams within casting distance of shore. Many anglers fishing shallow rivers combine shore fishing with shallow-water wading. Being able to fish from the middle of a stream lets you cast to more structure. Remember, most fish face the flow of water and wait for food to come to them.

Fishing the Surf

Surf fishing is a special type of shore fishing. Surf anglers either fish from the shore or wade into the shallow waters along the coasts. Usually, there's little visible structure, so surf fishermen must learn to "read" the water to detect shallow sloughs, pockets, tide rips, and other areas where fish may be present.

Piers

Fishing piers are structures that extend into the water for a few dozen feet or as much as several

hundred feet. Piers may be just above the surface or as much as 20 to 30 feet above the water. Piers let anglers get their baits and lures farther out into the water than a cast from the shore would allow.

Often a pier is built with rock piles or other structure next to it to attract fish. Even if this structure is absent, the pier pilings attract fish. Some of the best fishing is often right under a pier.

Breakwaters and Jetties

Breakwaters and jetties are similar to piers; they, too, extend into the water and offer a platform from which to fish. Most are built to protect harbor areas and boat slips from the wave action of the open ocean or a lake. Those designed for fishing have rocks arranged so that they're flat on top. When fishing breakwaters and jetties that aren't flat on top, use extra caution.

Walkways and Bridges

Walkways are like piers, but are specially built fishing platforms that are near or run parallel to bridges, piers, shoreline bulkheads, or similar structures. An example is a walkway along a bridge, but constructed at a lower level. This keeps anglers safe from auto traffic and puts them closer to the water.

Fishing isn't always allowed from bridges because of the danger from traffic. Bridges where angling is permitted must be fished carefully.

SHORE FISHING TACKLE

In most cases, tackle for shore fishing is no different from that used in fishing from a boat under the same conditions and for the same species of fish. Freshwater tackle is usually light for sunfish, small catfish, trout, smallmouth bass in streams, suckers, and small walleye. Medium tackle is used for largemouth bass, smallmouth bass in lakes, northern pike, carp, large catfish, and salmon. Heavy tackle is used for large salmon and trout, muskies, striped bass, and large carp.

Surf-fishing tackle is larger than that used for freshwater fishing because the fish are often bigger. Weights used to keep baits or lures on or near the bottom in currents and moving tides are also heavier. Medium to heavy tackle is used. A typical surf-fishing outfit consists of a large spinning reel with 12- to 20-pound test line and a heavy 8- to 12-foot rod. Long rods allow you to cast farther. Surf anglers usually use live bait until fish are visible. Then they switch to lures.

APPROACHING FISH

Fish are wary creatures. This is especially true in shallow water near the shore. Anglers must walk carefully because vibrations from their footsteps can be transmitted to the water and sensed by fish, spooking them away.

Vibration is less of a problem when fishing rivers and streams because the water's current conceals most bank vibrations.

When wading, avoid dislodging rocks that might make sounds that scare fish. Vibration isn't a problem when fishing from breakwaters, jetties, and piers.

When you fish still waters, these tips will

help you avoid being seen by fish. You should stay as low as possible, stay close to shrubbery, and wear dark or camouflage clothing. These are important since fish near the surface can easily detect movement on shore.

HOOKING AND LANDING FISH

Setting the Hook

"Setting the hook" refers to the method of forcing a hook into a fish's mouth.

In most cases, one sharp snap of the rod is all that is needed, provided the hook is sharp. Some situations, however, require more force than others. For example, a single hard strike is needed when using a soft-plastic worm rigged Texas style (the hook is concealed inside the worm) because the strike must drive the hook through the worm first and then into the fish's mouth. Striking too hard or repeatedly with a soft-mouthed fish such as a crappie, shad, or sea trout can pull the hook through the mouth.

Setting the Hook

Fighting a Fish

When a fish feels the hook, it struggles to get free. This might involve jumping, making a long run, swimming back into snags, or swimming around obstacles. Each species of fish fights differently. Some experienced anglers can often tell what species of fish is on the end of the line just by the way it fights. Carp, bonefish, and chinook salmon are strong, powerful fish that tend to make long runs. Largemouth bass and steelhead trout both run and jump. Tuna dive for the bottom. Trout and tarpon fight wildly when first hooked. Northern pike and cobia (ling) often come to the boat easily, but fight strongly near the boat. Sunfish zig-zag toward cover to take full advantage of their body shape.

Fish hooked and played in shallow water are more likely to jump and behave more frantically those hooked in deep water. When hooked, deep-water fish often seek the bottom. Large bass are less likely to jump than smaller bass.

It's possible to land many small fish just by reeling them in. They'll fight, but this can be easily overcome by the strength of the line and the fishing rod. Much of the enjoyment of fishing, though, is gained by using lighter tackle that allows the fish to fight. However, if you plan to release the fish, do not fight it so long that it becomes exhausted and later dies.

Fighting larger fish requires a technique called "pumping the rod." To do this, retrieve line quickly as you lower the rod until it is horizontal and pointed at the fish. Then stop retrieving line and slowly raise the rod up. When the rod is at about the 11 o'clock position, repeat the process until the fish is near and ready to be landed. Never let the line go slack in the process.

Landing a Fish

Fish can be landed by hand or with landing tools such as a net.

When you fish from the shore, beaching fish is a popular way to land them. This method, however, should only be used if you plan to keep and eat the fish because it will harm the coating on its body.

To beach a fish, lead it into increasingly shallower water, gradually sliding the fish on its side onto dry land. In saltwater, time your retrieve with an incoming wave. As the wave recedes, quickly grab your beached fish and pull it ashore.

Landing nets are commonly used for landing fish. Long-handled nets are used for boat or shore fishing and fishing from docks and jetties. Short-handled nets are used for stream fishing. The size of the net depends on the size of the fish you plan to catch. Some people use a circular net with a long rope instead of a handle; this is used for pier and bridge fishing.

Pumping the Rod

To net a fish, you must first have the fish under control as much as possible. Next, lead the fish to the net. Place the net in the water and lead the fish into the net head first. Then if the fish should try to escape, it will swim into the net. Once the fish is completely in the net, raise the net by the handle. If you have a heavy fish, also grasp the net's rim to prevent the handle from bending or breaking.

A popular way to land bass is by hand. Carefully avoiding hooks, many bass anglers use the thumb and index finger to grip a bass by its lower jaw. This holds the jaw wide open and temporarily paralyzes the fish. This makes hook removal easier.

To handle a fish with sharp teeth such as walleye or northern pike, carefully hold it around the body. Never hold a fish by the eyes or gills if you plan to free it. Other fish like chinook or Atlantic salmon have a strong tail and you can grasp them in front of the tail fin.

SAFETY

Fishing from shore isn't dangerous, but safe fishing requires common sense. In addition to following the safety precautions in Chapter 2, "Fishing Safely," there are a few other things you need to be aware of.

- Wear some type of footwear like a tennis shoe to protect you from glass and sharp objects.
- Wear a personal flotation device and use a wading stick or staff to help keep you from falling.
- River banks can erode making them unstable. Watch out for these unstable areas and stay away from them.
- Watch for rising water levels below dams or during incoming tides. Waters can rise quickly, trapping you away from shore.
- Rocks, muddy banks, and downed trees can be slick, making it easy to slip.
- Rocks and downed trees can also turn when you step on them, making you fall.
- When fishing from an area where there are lots of people, be particularly careful when casting. You want to catch fish, not other anglers.

GET PERMISSION

Although many shore fishing locations are for public use, others are not. Always get permission to fish on private property and pay attention to any special requests or regulations of the land-owner. Make sure all gates are left as you found them (open or closed). Do not walk through crops or livestock. Help to keep the place clean and offer to share your catch with the land-owner.

ACTIVITIES

ACTIVITY 1 — TESTING YOUR PFD

Personal flotation devices are needed while fishing, but many people have never been in the water with one on. Obtain a PFD, and go to a local swimming area or pool with an adult. Make sure the PFD is on securely, and jump in. Try to go underwater; try floating on your back and swimming a short distance.

If you ever do have an accident and must rely on a PFD, this experience will help.

ACTIVITY 2 — HOW DOES A FISH SENSE VIBRATIONS?

Bang a tuning fork or gravy stirrer against one hand and feel the vibrations in the hand holding it. Fish feel objects that "bang" the water because they create vibrations that fish feel through the line of cells in their lateral line. How effective do you think the lateral line in a fish might be?

ACTIVITY 3 — SELECTING FISHING EQUIPMENT

Using fishing magazines and catalogs, cut out the pictures of the equipment you need to begin fishing from shore. Pretend that your have $100.00 to purchase your equipment. Paste the pictures of your equipment selections onto posterboard or construction paper. Write the cost of each piece of equipment and add up the total cost. Did you stay within your budget?

ACTIVITY 4 — SETTING THE HOOK

It is important that you learn how to set the hook. Before you learn to set the hook you must remember to keep slack out of your line. If there is slack in your line you will not be able to properly set the hook and you will lose a lot of fish.

When you feel a fish bite or strike your bait, quickly lower the tip of your rod and at the same time reel up the slack line. When your rod is pointing at the water, quickly snap the rod upward, keeping your hands in front of you and your elbows close to your body so that you remain in control. Begin reeling immediately.

To practice this, tie the end of your line to some immovable object. Back away from the object about 20 feet. Pretend that you have a strike, lower your rod while reeling up the slack, and with a quick snap of your wrists raise the rod to set the hook.

ACTIVITY 5 — FIGHTING A LARGE FISH BY PUMPING THE ROD

Sometimes when you hook a large fish you cannot just reel it in. At these times you must know how to pump the rod to land your fish.

To pump the rod effectively, you must again remember to keep your elbows next to your body and not lift your hands over your head. After you have set your hook, raise the rod tip to a vertical position, then slowly lower the rod reeling in line as you lower the rod. When the rod reaches a horizontal position, stop reeling and again lift the rod to a vertical position, keeping your elbows close to your body. Repeat this process over and over until the fish is close enough to land.

To practice pumping the rod, tie your line to some object weighing approximately five pounds. Back away about 20 feet and take the slack out of the line. Raise the rod by pulling the tip up, and then, keeping the line tight without any slack, lower the rod reeling as you go, and then lift the rod again. The object you have your line tied to will come closer to you each time you raise your rod.

ACTIVITY 6 — KEEPING A FISHING LOG BOOK

Each time you go fishing record the following information in a special notebook:

Date fished—
Place fished—
Number and kind of fish caught—
Types of lures or bait used—
Weather conditions—
Time when fishing was best—
Who fished with you—

It is helpful to keep a record of your fishing trips so that you can look back to check on your success under different fishing conditions. This can help you become a more successful angler.

CHAPTER
5
Fishing From Boats

Fishing from a boat allows you to cover a larger part of a body of water than shore fishing. In their simplest form, boats can be nothing more than a platform that you sit or stand on. Some boats are made for rivers and streams, for small lakes, or for large bodies of water. Oars or paddles, electric motors, or gasoline motors move them through the water. Boats are made of wood, metal, fiberglass, rubber, and other materials.

Some boats used for fishing include canoes, skiffs, jonboats, V-hull boats, cathedral-hull boats, and specialty boats.

If you decide to try fishing from a boat, there is a lot to know before you go. You need to know about:

- The boat and how it handles.
- The equipment on the boat and how it works.
- The waters you will be boating on and any hazards such as submerged trees and rocks.
- The weather conditions and emergency procedures.
- The safety devices on the boat and how they work.
- Your own personal abilities-how much you know-how much you can do before you become too tired.

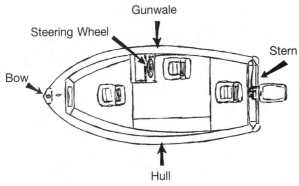

As the operator of a boat you are legally responsible for the boat and the safety of those on board. You must also understand the rules of navigation and the courtesies of safe boating. Always complete a boater safety course prior to operating a boat for the first time.

WAYS TO MOVE BOATS

Pole, Paddles, and Oars

Long poles can be used to move a small boat in shallow water. Paddles are mainly used with a canoe, but many states require that a paddle or pair of oars be part of a boat's emergency equipment. Oars can be used to move a boat on small bodies of water.

Electric Motor

A battery-powered electric motor can be used to move a small boat slowly on small ponds or on lakes. An electric motor is also often used on boats with outboard motors. The outboard is used to reach a fishing spot quickly. Then, the electric motor is used to control the boat's position while fishing.

Outboard Motor

An outboard motor is a gasoline engine mounted on a boat's stern, the back of the boat. Outboards range from one-horsepower to large engines of 200 horsepower or more. You control small outboards with a steering handle, often called a tiller. Large outboards are controlled with a steering wheel.

Inboard Engine

An inboard motor is completely inside the boat.

Inboard engines can run on gasoline or diesel fuel and are usually found on boats 18 feet or longer.

HANDLING A BOAT

Learning how to use a boat safely is very important.

Steering

On a smaller boat with an outboard motor, the motor's handle is used to steer the boat. Since the engine is mounted on the rear of the boat, it pushes the stern around, making the bow go in the opposite direction.

To turn starboard (right), move the handle to the left. To turn port (left), move the handle to the right. On larger boats with an outboard or inboard motor, a steering wheel is used to steer, much like driving a car.

Speed

The speed of a boat depends upon both the size of the motor and the boat. The speed of the motor is controlled by a throttle. This throttle has the same purpose as the gas pedal on a car.

Gearshift

The smallest outboard motors have no gearshift. The boat moves as soon the engine is started. Larger motors have a gearshift lever. There are three positions—forward, neutral, and reverse. Place the lever into neutral to start the engine. Then, when it's running, you put the lever in forward or reverse gear to move forward or backward.

Placing the shift lever in neutral will not stop the boat. Since a boat does not have brakes you must learn to judge your speed and maneuver carefully using the forward and reverse controls to avoid hitting docks and other boats or objects.

FLOAT PLAN

Always let someone know where you are going, the water course you plan to take and when you plan to return. In an emergency this can save your life!

BOATING LAWS

Anglers using boats must obey boating laws. A boat must have emergency equipment on board. For example, a **U.S. Coast Guard-approved personal flotation device (PFD) is required for each person on board.** Other equipment depends on the type and length of the boat.

> **To boat safely:**
> - Successfully complete a boating safety course.
> - Never operate a boat while under the influence of alcohol or drugs.
> - Drive at a safe speed.
> - Operate a boat outside of protected or swimming areas.
> - Operate a ski boat away from swimmers or anglers.
> - Keep out of the path of larger vessels and sailboats.
> - Remain seated. Stand up only if necessary. Always wear your PFD.
> - Anchor outside of a shipping channel.
> - Do not overload a boat with too many passengers or too much equipment.
> - Use navigation lights at night.
> - Use an outboard motor that is the right size for the boat.

Boaters also must follow the "Rules of the Road," which include knowing which boat has the right-of-way. However, sailboats have the right-of-way over power boats. The U.S. Navigation Rules include:

- Boats approaching each other **must stay to the right at all times and pass each other port (left) side to port side.**

- You can overtake another boat on either side, but you must use caution so that your boat's wake does not endanger the boat being passed.

- When boats approach at an angle, the boat on the starboard (right) side has the right of way and must hold its course and speed. The other boat must keep clear and pass behind the boat with the right of way.

STORMS

Boating during a storm can be dangerous, especially when there is lightning, strong wind or high waves. The first thing to do is make sure everyone is wearing a PFD. Put all fishing rods in the bottom of the boat. Stay low or lie down in the boat to reduce the risk of capsizing. Get off the water as soon as you can.

Don't fish during an electrical storm. Anglers are killed every year when their rods or boats are hit by lightning.

If you can't get off the water, try to prevent waves from coming in over the stern or striking the boat on its side. The best way is to keep the boat moving at a slight angle into the waves. Moving with the waves can be dangerous. They can come in over the transom and fill the boat with water. This could sink the boat.

If you have no choice and must ride out a storm on the water, use a heavy anchor with a long line attached to the bow of the boat. The anchor line needs to be at least seven times the depth of the water so that the anchor can hold to the bottom. If the anchor drags, make sure that the boat is not pulled into rocks, shallow water, or rougher water.

EQUIPMENT AND STORAGE

A boat should always be kept tidy. Life-saving gear must be stored where it can be reached quickly. Gasoline containers should be placed in the stern and clamped in brackets or held down with cords. Anchors should be stowed in the bow with the anchor line coiled neatly for instant use.

doesn't move around or blow out when the boat is under way.

Learn to use a compass correctly, and then always carry one on board because fog, rain, or darkness can cause you to lose your way.

EMERGENCIES

By staying alert and watching out for other people and potentially hazardous situations, you can avoid conditions that cause boats to sink or capsize. Many accidents are caused by speeding, unsafe turns, overloading the boat, or hitting an underwater object. Capsizing and people falling overboard cause many life-threatening situations. Everyone should wear a PFD at all times.

If someone falls overboard, throw a PFD with a line attached. Then, carefully bring the boat to the person, stopping the engine when near the person in the water. Maneuvering a boat into position and pulling someone out of the water without capsizing the vessel is very difficult. Review Chapter 2 to learn the correct procedure.

Every boat with a gasoline engine should have at least one fire extinguisher. It should be a Coast Guard-approved extinguisher for electrical and gasoline fires. Keep it where it can be reached quickly, near the stern of the boat, but not too close to the engine.

Batteries should be stored in battery boxes and have their terminals covered to prevent electrical shorting and fires. All other gear, including fishing tackle, should be stored so that it

Methods of Fishing
from Boats

35

BOAT READINESS CHECKLIST

A checklist is a good way to make sure your boat is ready for use. Your checklist should include the following items:

- **Fishing License.** A fishing license, where required, must be carried while fishing.
- **Boat Registration.** Boat registrations, when required, must be carried while using a boat.
- **Fuel.** A boat's fuel tank should be filled before each trip. Use the 1/3 rule—use 1/3 of your fuel for the trip out, 1/3 for the trip back, and keep 1/3 in reserve in case of an emergency. Always clean up any spilled gasoline.
- **Fire Extinguisher.** A boat should be equipped with at least one Coast Guard-approved fire extinguisher.
- **Lights.** A boat used at night must have operating navigation lights. Navigation lights are a red (port) light, a green (starboard) light, and a white stern or masthead light. Check to make sure they're working.
- **Personal Flotation Devices.** PFDs are required on all boats and some boats also must have at least one PFD that can be thrown to a person in the water. Wear your PFD and make sure that it fits properly. Test it in a pool or swimming area to ensure that it will float you with the clothing that you would normally wear when fishing.

- **Paddle or Oars.** Since motors tend to break down at the worst times, oars or a paddle are an absolute must for emergency use.
- **Lines.** Lines are not legally required, but are necessary for docking, anchoring, mooring, or towing.
- **Other Items.** Other items that may be included in a BOATERS' DUFFEL BAG are:
  - VHF-FM Radio
  - Chart and Compass
  - Rope and Throw Bag
  - Visual Distress Signals
  - Bailer (can, scoop, bucket)
  - Binoculars
  - Food and Water
  - Medical Supplies
    - First-Aid Kit
    - Special Medications
    - Sunblock (SPF 15, at least)
  - Tool Kit
  - Whistle or Horn
  - Extra Clothing
    - Sunglasses
    - Sun Hat
    - Rain Gear
    - Wool Sweater
    - Stocking Cap
    - Gloves

The Coast Guard Auxiliary, the United States Power Squadron, and some state agencies offer courtesy boat examinations to see that a boat has the required safety equipment on board.

DON'T SPREAD AQUATIC WEEDS

All weeds should be removed from a boat and trailer before launching. Weeds such as milfoil can be spread from lake to lake by boaters. Milfoil can ruin fishing by spreading rapidly, interfering with boating access. The excess vegetation can also protect too many small fish which causes overpopulation. In addition, when these weeds die, they decompose, removing oxygen from the water, creating low-oxygen conditions that can cause fish to die.

COURTESY ON THE WATER

Common sense and courtesy makes everyone's day on the water safer and more enjoyable.

People go boating to have fun and fun can only come if everyone's rights are respected and all rules of boat and water safety are obeyed.

ACTIVITIES

ACTIVITY 1 — WHERE CAN I GO FISHING?

Obtain a book about your state which lists bodies of water where public fishing is allowed. This book should also tell the specific regulations for each body of water. Your local sporting goods store or your local conservation officer should have copies of this book.

Make a chart placing the names of the bodies of water in your area that you will want to fish along the left side of the chart. Using these column headings: (1) open season, (2) types of boats allowed, (3) types and sizes of engines allowed, (4) speed limits, (5) size restrictions for different species of fish, (6) other information of your choice, write in the appropriate information for each body of water.

As you continue to fish, new categories can be added such as number of fish caught, species caught, bait used, time of day, season, water temperature, etc. This information can be very valuable as you continue angling.

ACTIVITY 2 — LOADING YOUR BOAT

Boat safety depends on how much weight is in the boat and how it is arranged. Cut a half-gallon cardboard milk carton in half lengthways, and throw away the half with the pouring spout. Using the other half, try loading it with some form of weight such as stones, nails or something similar. How much can your "milk boat" handle? What happens when you pile your weights at one end? What does this tell you about the importance of balancing the load in your boat?

ACTIVITY 3 — WHY WOODEN BOATS HOLD WATER

Older boats were made of wood, and after being stored over the winter or for long periods out of the water they could leak badly when put into the water. They would stop leaking, however, after being in the water for a while. This activity may help explain why they quit leaking.

Fill a glass container 1/2 full of dry beans. Fill the container to the top with water. Mark the level of the beans with a piece of tape and put the container out of the way until the next morning.

Examine the container. Compare the level of the beans with the tape. Is the level of the beans higher or lower? How about the water level? Why are they different? Did the beans soak up the water? Does this help you to understand why the boat stopped leaking.

ACTIVITY 4 — BOATS FOR DIFFERENT USES

Collect pictures of boats used for different types of fishing. Under each boat tell what type of fishing you would use the boat for and what equipment would be needed to meet safety regulations in your state.

Paste on a piece of poster board and label the parts of each boat with their proper names.

6

A Good Angler Is . . . .

As an angler you have an important responsibility. It's much more than obeying fishing laws. Good anglers also respect others and the resource. Your actions will allow many other people to enjoy fishing in the future.

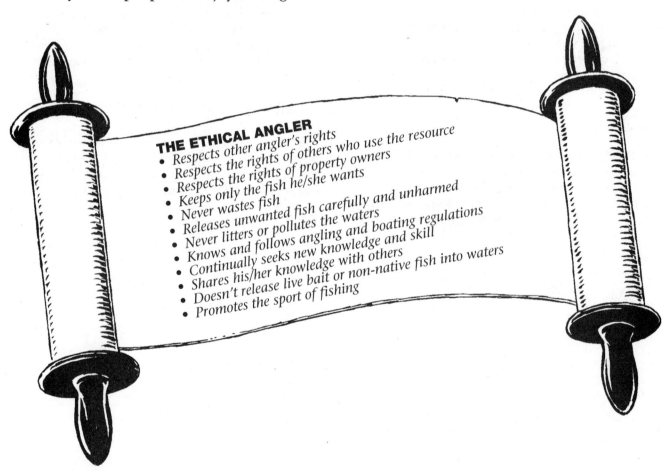

THE ETHICAL ANGLER
- Respects other angler's rights
- Respects the rights of others who use the resource
- Respects the rights of property owners
- Keeps only the fish he/she wants
- Never wastes fish
- Releases unwanted fish carefully and unharmed
- Never litters or pollutes the waters
- Knows and follows angling and boating regulations
- Continually seeks new knowledge and skill
- Shares his/her knowledge with others
- Doesn't release live bait or non-native fish into waters
- Promotes the sport of fishing

RESPECT FOR OTHERS

Respect For Other Anglers

Anglers respect the rights of others. Some people may enjoy sitting on the bank of a pond and fishing peacefully. Others may prefer using a boat to catch fish. You can fish the way you like and not judge how someone else chooses to fish. Following the **Golden Rule** is a good plan: treat other anglers as you would like to be treated.

For example, if you were fishing would you like to have another angler start fishing too close to you? You would probably be angry because the other angler was crowding you! If you left your spot to land a fish, you would feel that you had the right to return to your original fishing spot. When we respect the rights of others as we enjoy fishing it makes the day more pleasant for everyone.

Respect For Non-Anglers

Some people use our water resources for activities other than fishing. Respect their right to use the area.

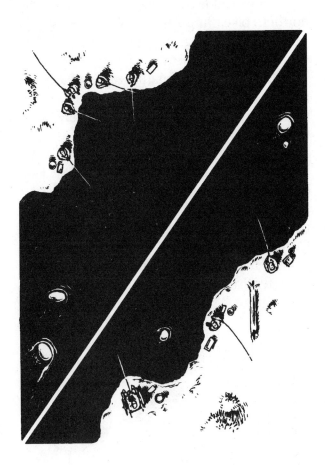

Respect For Land-owners

You may not always be fishing on public waters. If you have to cross someone's land to get to the water, always ask the landowner for permission first. If you want to fish privately owned waters, always ask permission from the land-owner before fishing. This is true whether or not the land is posted. If you have to go through gates, be sure to leave them as you found them. If you opened the gate, close it immediately. Do not litter! Leave the area cleaner than you found it. If you catch some fish from the landowner's pond, offer to share your catch with them. Doing these things is a good way to get an invitation to come back.

RESPECT FOR THE RESOURCE

Good anglers respect our country's water resources. These resources need to be protected so others can enjoy them. We all share this responsibility.

Never Litter

Never leave any litter behind. If you walk to a fishing spot, *carry out everything* you carry in. This includes ...food wrappers, old fishing line, bait holders, empty cans or bottles and plastic bags. Pick up litter left behind by others, too. It is easy to carry a small paper bag for this purpose. If you are fishing from a boat, be sure your litter is put into a closed container so it can't blow out of the boat. If we all do these things our lakes and streams will be much cleaner.

Picking Up Litter

Sinking empty soda cans or bottles is worse than leaving them on shore. You are littering the bottom of the lake. Carry empty containers when you leave your fishing spot and recycle them.

Never Waste Fish

Good anglers know that fish are food and should never be wasted. Never keep more fish than you can use. If you catch a fish that's too small to eat or one that's under the legal or minimum size, it should be released quickly and carefully. Releasing a fish and watching it swim away unharmed is a wonderful feeling. If you want to show your fish to others, take a picture before releasing it. The picture will bring you many fond memories and the fish can bring enjoyment to another angler.

To release a fish, keep it in the water if you can. Handle it carefully with a wet hand so it can be released unharmed. If it's a fish without sharp teeth like a bass, hold its lower lip between your thumb and index finger. If it has sharp teeth like a walleye or northern pike, carefully hold it around the body. Never hold a fish by the eyes or gills if it is to be released.

Tearing a hook out can harm the fish so badly that it may not live. If the fish is hooked deeply and the hook can't easily be removed, cut the line to release the fish. The hook will rust, dissolve, or become loose without harming the fish. The use of barbless hooks makes it easier to release fish.

If a fish loses consciousness, try to revive it by **gently** moving it in a figure-eight pattern so water moves through its gills. When the fish begins to struggle and can swim, let it go.

Today, some species of fish exist in limited numbers. More and more anglers know this and participate in "catch and release" fishing. Now, many anglers take only what they need for food and release the rest unharmed. This makes it possible for other anglers to enjoy catching them again.

Some fish take longer to become adults and may not spawn (lay their eggs) until they are three to seven years old. Then, they spawn only once a year. You should release many of these fish. They include bass, lake trout, muskellunge, northern pike, sturgeon, walleye, and most large gamefish. Catching and then releasing these species is a good practice.

Other fish species mature earlier and spawn more than once a year. For example, bluegill and many other panfish spawn when they are two to three years old.

Until recently, few anglers realized that the populations of certain gamefish in the large oceans could become threatened. However, to increase fish populations, fish hatcheries are raising and stocking fish in the Atlantic and Pacific Oceans and the Gulf of Mexico. Today, redfish, snook, seatrout, striped bass, and other saltwater fish are being raised for stocking.

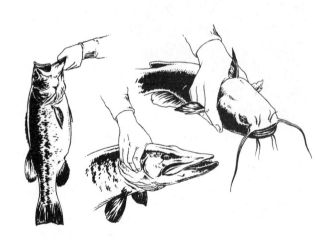

Protect The Area Around The Waters

Never destroy the beauty of an area. Do not spray paint or carve names or other words on rocks or trees. Do not drive through streams and riparian areas. Leave wildflowers and other plants growing in the wild. Do not destroy or pick them.

Continually Seek New Knowledge and Skill

A good angler is always trying to learn more. . . increasing fishing skills, learning more about the behavior of fish, and learning more about the harmful things people do to the resource. In this way, you can become part of the solution-not part of the problem. You don't have to know it all now; you will learn something each trip.

Share Knowledge

Good anglers share their knowledge with others and introduce their friends to the sport of fishing and the benefits of protecting the environment.

Know And Follow Fishing Regulations

Fishing laws are meant to protect the resource and make sure there is fishing to be shared by everyone. If you fish, it's important that you know the rules and regulations. Ignorance of the law is no excuse. Fishing is a wonderful privilege; obeying fishing regulations is the responsibility that goes with it.

If there are fishing seasons, you must know them. Seasons protect fish during spawning and limit the catch on heavily fished waters. Limits on the number of fish that can be caught are meant to keep anglers from taking too many fish at one time. This makes it possible for more people to share the resource.

Report Violators

Anglers also have a responsibility to help state agencies protect our natural resources. Today, many states have a special telephone number so individuals can report those who violate fish and game laws.

Participate in Resource-Enhancement Projects

A good angler gets involved in projects to enhance the resource. Some students do it as a class project. Others join or form clubs whose members will work on projects such as improving a stretch of water on a stream, building fish structure in lakes, or just cleaning up the bank around a lake, stream, or river.

41

ACTIVITIES

ACTIVITY 1 — WHAT CAN I DO TO ENHANCE THE RESOURCE?

Design and draw a fishing scene that shows one or more examples of how to be a good angler. These examples may give you some ideas.

1. Picking up litter.
2. Showing respect for fellow anglers.
3. Showing courtesy to non-anglers using the water for recreation.
4. Helping a beginning angler.
5. Showing respect for wildlife.
6. Showing respect for private property where you are fishing.
7. Following fishing regulations.

ACTIVITY 2 — HELP CATCH A POACHER

Design and create an attractive poster that informs anglers about fishing violations and how to report violators. Obtain permission from local area bait, sporting or fishing shops to display your poster throughout the season.

ACTIVITY 3 — ADOPT A POND

Take an active part in eliminating trash from your favorite water resource. Adopt part or all of a local pond or stream. Adopting means that you assume responsibility for this area all of the time. During your fishing time or during periodic checks, pick up all trash that you can safely reach.

Enlist the help of friends. Talk to other anglers about adopting another area. Write the local newspaper urging similar actions from other anglers. If your pond or stream is heavily used and lacks a trash container, check with your local department of Natural Resources about a permanent trash barrel.

ACTIVITY 4 — WHAT IS BIODEGRADABLE?

Place some fishing line, a pop can tab, a hook and perhaps a plastic worm in a hole in your yard, garden or in a bucket filled with dirt or potting soil along with some vegetable peelings or material you have left from preparing your fish for cooking. Cover up your items and let them stay there undisturbed for six to nine months. Then dig them up and examine each item. Which items left in a pond will decay? Which will be left to litter the environment and perhaps cause harm to fish and other aquatic animals?

7

What Is Water?

Good anglers are concerned about the fish's primary need-WATER. You probably don't think much about water even though you use it everyday. Water is very important because there's nothing else like it in the world. Fish are not the only animals that could not live without it. We couldn't live without it and can't afford to take it for granted.

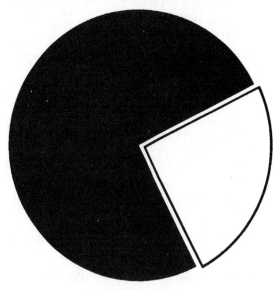

There is a lot of water. It covers about 70 percent of the earth, but only about three percent of it is fresh water. Most of the fresh water, about 75 percent, is in the form of ice. In fact, the frozen areas of the world have as much fresh water as all the world's rivers will carry for the next 1,000 years.

The demand for unpolluted fresh water is increasing because the earth's population is increasing. How much water does the average person use? Here are some answers:

- In the home, each person uses about 70 gallons of water a day.
- It takes three gallons to flush a toilet.
- It takes 15 to 30 gallons to take a bath.

- It takes five gallons for a one-minute shower.
- It takes ten gallons to wash dishes.

This is a lot of water, but more than half of the water used in the United States is used by industries. For example, it takes 250 tons of water to make a ton of newspaper and ten gallons to produce one gallon of gasoline. You can see why it is important to conserve water.

SHARING WATERS

As you have seen, anglers and boaters are not the only ones who use bodies of water and have an effect on fish populations. Industries and power plants use large amounts of water. Communities need water for drinking. Farmers use it to water their crops and livestock. Barges and ships use waterways to bring products to market. Water is also used for waste disposal.

The demands for water use can cause conflicts among those using our water resources. The results are not always good for the fish and not everyone is concerned with fish.

An occasional conflict arises when people want to dam a river for irrigation, for controlling floods, or for the production of electricity. Dams create lakes or reservoirs that are habitat for fish such as largemouth bass and crappie. However, the reservoir destroys several miles of river that might have been prime habitat for trout, smallmouth or rock bass.

Water is too valuable to waste. With so much demand for our water it is important that each of us do our part to conserve it.:

How You Can Conserve Water

- Reducing water use in the kitchen and bathroom.
- Shutting the water off between rinsing dishes or brushing our teeth.
- Turning the water on only when we are actually using it.
- Taking showers since they use less water than baths.
- Using flow-restricting devices on shower heads.
- Fixing leaky faucets.
- Running only full loads of clothes in the washer.
- Placing a plastic bottle or brick in the water tank of the toilet so that it will use less water for each flushing.
- Not using water for watering lawns or washing cars during times of water shortage.

FACTS ABOUT WATER

How Much Water Is There? The bad news is that there is a limited amount of water on earth. **In fact, there's no more water today than there was when the earth was formed.** The good news is that water is recycled. Over time, it's used over and over again. Because of this, it's important not to pollute water so that it can be used safely by humans, fish, and other life forms that depend on it.

The Water Cycle

The heat from the sun causes water on the earth to evaporate, or turn into a vapor, and rise into the air. As this vapor rises, it cools, condenses into water droplets and forms clouds. Sooner or later, the water returns to earth in the form of rain, snow, sleet or hail.

When water strikes the earth, some of it returns to vapor through evaporation. Some of it enters brooks, creeks, streams, and rivers. Eventually, this water makes its way into the oceans. Water also seeps into the ground, becoming groundwater. It moves slowly until it reaches rivers or lakes or drains into large underground areas called aquifers.

The Water Cycle

Water Is A Solvent

Water is often called the "universal solvent." This is because water can dissolve so many things. Water can dissolve some things like salt and sugar very quickly. Other materials may take thousands or even millions of years to dissolve. For example, flowing water can dissolve rock. That, along with other types of erosion, is how the Grand Canyon and other canyons and river valleys were formed.

Boiling And Freezing Points

Water turns into ice at a temperature of 32 degrees F, 0 degrees C. It boils at a temperature of 212 degrees F, 100 degrees C, and turns into a gas or vapor. It is a liquid between 32 and 212 degrees F and 0 and 100 degrees C. Water also has the ability to store a large amount of heat. This is important because it means that water heats and cools more slowly than land or air.

An angler should know about water temperature. In spring, water temperature rises very slowly. Water warms and cools more slowly than air. Although the air temperature may be warm, the water in some areas may still be too cold for some kinds of fish. Late in the year, the opposite may be true. In fall, water temperature drops very slowly. The air may be chilly, but the water temperature may still be warm. Fish are more active in warmer water than in cold water. Thus, when fishing in colder water, anglers should work their baits and retrieve line more slowly.

Why Ice Floats

Another interesting fact is that cold water is not always heavier than warm water. Water continues to get heavier as it cools, until it reaches a temperature of 39.2 degrees F. At this temperature, one cubic foot of water weighs more than 62 pounds. Then, something unusual happens. Water colder than 39 degrees F begins to get lighter. No other liquid acts this way.

What does this mean to us? Well, if water colder than 39 degrees F did not get lighter, ice wouldn't float. Instead, ice would form on the bottom of a lake and kill fish and other life in the water. The fact that water gets lighter before it freezes is important in deep northern lakes.

Turnover

As the sun melts ice on a lake in spring and begins to heat the surface water, a change takes place. When the surface water begins to warm, it sinks to the bottom, helped by wind and currents. This pushes colder water from the bottom toward the surface. This mixing of water is called "turnover." Turnover often occurs in the spring and fall. After the turnover, the water temperature of the mixed water is nearly the same throughout the lake. During this period fish are likely to be scattered and at any depth.

Turnover

Water Layers

In summer, however, something else occurs on many deep or large lakes. The water forms three layers, each with a different range of temperatures. The sun warms the top layer (**epilimnion**) of water faster than the wind can mix it. Another layer (**hypolimnion**) is the heavy cold water at the bottom of the lake. This layer may have very little oxygen. The third layer is a narrow one that separates the top and bottom layers, called the "metalimnione," and contains a **thermocline.** Here the water temperature changes rapidly with only small changes in depth.

Why is knowing about these layers important? One reason is that the bottom layer in some lakes has little oxygen. This forces fish to move to a higher level and into the metalimnion, near the thermocline. So in summer on lakes that separate into layers, fish will frequently move to the epilimnion to feed and then return to their preferred temperatures near the thermocline.

Freshwater lakes are not the only places where water forms into layers. It also happens in saltwater estuaries and in the oceans.

Water layers

WATER QUALITY

We need to make sure that we keep our waters clean and free from pollution. For fish and other animals to live and thrive, the quality of water is very important.

When harmful things enter our waters, the waters become polluted. Polluted water cannot be used for drinking, swimming, or fishing. The key lies in eliminating pollution. Fortunately, **you can make a difference!** In the next chapter you will learn about different types of pollution. You will also learn how you can become part of the solution instead of part of the problem.

If water is kept clean and used wisely, there will be enough for our many needs.

ACTIVITIES

ACTIVITY 1 — THE WATER CYCLE

Fill half of a large metal tray with water and place in a freezer. Remove the tray when the water is frozen. With an adult's help, heat a half-filled pot of water to a boil. Place a small wire grate over the pan and put your frozen tray on the grate. Observe the following: 1. Evaporation of water, by heat as the level of the heated water goes down; 2. Formation of water vapor above boiling water; 3. Water droplets forming on the cold surface of the frozen tray; and 4. Accumulation of droplets that form

and fall from the underside of the frozen tray. Relate what you observe to the water cycle present on earth. The heat of the stove represents the heat of the sun's energy.

ACTIVITY 2 — OIL AND EGGS DON'T MIX

Chicken eggs are similar to fish eggs. Both have a porous covering that allows gases to enter and leave the egg. Place a fresh chicken egg in a two-cup liquid measurer almost full of water. Notice the bubbles forming on the egg's surface. Let it sit for five minutes and check it again. Gently tap the side of the cup. What happens to the bubbles? Now take your egg out and dry it completely. Cover it with vegetable oil or lard. Place it back in the water. What difference in bubble formation do you see? What might happen to fish eggs in an oil spill?

ACTIVITY 3 — WATCHING TURNOVER

Fill a 9- X 13-inch pyrex or other ceramic, heat-resistant dish with water. At one end place a small plastic bag filled with ice. Carefully add some boiling water in the end opposite the bag of ice. Place several drops of green or blue food coloring next to the bag of ice. Watch where the drop of dye goes. Add a drop next to the warm water. What happens to this dye? The cold water sinks and the warm moves over the surface. This is what happens as turnover in a pond in the spring. The opposite happens in the fall. Water colder than 39.2 degrees F rises, creating another period of turnover.

ACTIVITY 4 — A LOT OF WATER DOWN THE DRAIN

Below are the estimated populations for the years 1990 and 1995. If each of these persons will use 70 gallons daily, then how much water will be used daily in 1900? in 1995? If your mind is warmed up, try this problem. What is the total water amount that might be used for one week in the year 1990? 1995?

Year	Population
1990	249,657,000
1995	259,559,000

ACTIVITY 5 — CHANGE IN WATER TEMPERATURE

Fill a pint cardboard milk container with room-temperature water. Leave an inch of space at the top. Fill a half-gallon carton with room-temperature water, leaving about two inches of space at the top. Have another pint container filled only with room-temperature air. Put a safe, breakproof thermometer in each. Put lids on each container or cover the tops with aluminum foil. Put the containers outside on a very cold day, in a refrigerator or freezer, or in a chest filled with ice. Every 15 minutes, record the time and the temperature in each container. Stop the experiment before the water freezes.

Which changes in temperature more slowly-a large body of water or a small one? Does water change temperature more slowly or does air?

ACTIVITY 6 — WHERE DOES ICE FORM?

Fill a paper cup with cold water, but leave about an inch of space at the top. Use a marker pen to draw a line on the cup at the top of the water. Freeze the water in the cup and study the line. If the water expands above the line and takes up more space in the cup, then it must be lighter or less dense that it was. Could this expansion explain why water freezing in a crack can break a rock or concrete?

8

The Problem With Pollution

Clean, pure water may be our most precious resource. Pollution is anything that spoils its cleanliness, purity, and overall quality. Many things that reduce the quality of the water pollute our ponds, lakes, streams, rivers, ground water and oceans.

Some, like gradual erosion of nearby land, occur naturally. However, uncontrolled development or careless farming methods increase ero-

sion and ruin waterways. Some pollutants enter our waters from the rain or air. Unfortunately, some pollution is even caused by thoughtless or uncaring people. Pollution is not only a danger to fish and other creatures that depend on clean water to live, but also to people!

Pollution problems may differ depending on where you live. In the northeastern U.S., acid rain may be the biggest threat to fish and other wildlife. Along Lake Superior, asbestos particles from mining waste has been a problem. Timber harvest in mountainous areas can cause erosion and sediment to flow into lakes and streams. Mercury is a concern in many lakes in Wisconsin and Minnesota. Around much of the Great Lakes, PCBs and other chemicals are a concern.

In most large urban communities, the main cause of water pollution is a combination of sewage and industrial waste. Unfortunately, some water can't be used because it is too polluted by chemical industrial waste. For instance, eight billion gallons of fresh water flow past the city of New York every day as the Hudson River empties into the Atlantic Ocean. That's enough water to supply each of 40 million people with 200 gallons a day if it could be used. The Hudson River, however, is too polluted to be used as a water supply.

To be a good angler you need to be familiar with the major kinds of pollution. When you are old enough to vote you will be asked to make decisions about proposed laws. You will want to be knowledgeable so you can make decisions that are healthy for the environment. No matter what age you are, you can always write your state legislator or congressional representative to express your views. Fish can't write, so they have to depend on you to make sure our waters remain clean.

Those who are concerned about water pollution use two terms—**point-source** and **non-point-source.**

Point-source pollution is pollution that can be traced to a definite point at which it enters the environment. Point-source pollution can come from industries that dump wastes, chemicals, or heavy metals into the environment. Toxic waste dumps

and waste water treatment plants are also point-source pollution sites.

Non-point-source pollution is more difficult to identify because it doesn't enter the water at a definite, easy-to-locate place. Often, it's caused by herbicides, pesticides, and fertilizers used on many lawns, farms, gardens and orchards and that eventually enter a waterway and harm the food chain.

TYPES OF POLLUTANTS

Silt Or Sediment

Have you ever seen a stream that looks dirty? This dirty look is usually caused by the excessive erosion of silt or sediments from nearby lands. Silt or sediment is fine particles of soil that end up in our waters. A small amount of sediment reaching the waters is natural. However, surface mining, timber harvest, construction, and poor farming practices can leave soil unstable. Then, when it rains, the soil is carried off by the water which eventually runs into a river or lake. There are modern methods of farming, logging, and mining that minimize erosion.

So, how can excessive silt hurt water? When it settles to the bottom it has a smothering effect. It can kill plants or other small organisms. It can smother fish eggs and young aquatic life. It can cover up the rocks where the fish's food lives. If the silt does not settle, the water ends up with a dirty look. This muddy water does not allow light for use by plants and other aquatic life. The result is a ruined body of water that no longer supports the fish we want to catch.

Agricultural Wastes

Agricultural wastes include manure, liquid and granular fertilizers, silo liquids and pesticides. Cattle, hogs, sheep and poultry raised on feed lots are a big problem. They concentrate a lot of wastes over a very small area. One cow produces as much waste as 17 people every day. Some of this waste is washed directly into rivers. In addition, farmers spread manure and fertilizer on their open fields that may eventually enter a body of water.

Pesticides are chemicals used to help farmers control pests that ruin their crops. If properly used they generally create little or no problem. However, when they enter a water system through careless use, they usually cause environmental damage by killing fish and other organisms in the water.

Acid Rain

Acid rain is one of the biggest problems facing the quality of our water today. Many bodies of water are suffering from the effects of acid rain. Acid rain is a result of industries and autos burning oil and coal (fossil fuels) for fuel. Industry smokestacks and automobile tailpipes send sulfur dioxide and nitrogen oxides high into the atmosphere. These elements can remain in the air for several days and travel hundreds of miles. While in the air they mix with water vapor and turn into sulfuric and nitric acids. Eventually, this harmful acid returns to earth in rain, hail, fog, dew, sleet, snow, or as dry particles. This acid damages plant life and may eventually kill insects, frogs, and fish in our waters.

The amount of acid in liquids is measured on a scale from 0 to 14. This is called the "pH" scale. A pH of 7.0 (distilled water) is in the middle of the scale and is considered neutral—neither acidic nor alkaline. Things below 7.0 such as lemon juice (pH of 2.0) are acidic. Things above 7.0, like ammonia (pH 11.0), are alkaline.

The pH scale is logarithmic. This means that a pH of 6 is *ten*

Acid Rain

Once a body of water contains too much acid, the creatures in the water's food chain begin to die. Eggs and larvae are sensitive to low pH and unable to survive. As water becomes more acid, the fertility of eggs is reduced, fewer hatch, and fish may not grow to adult sizes. Eventually, fish or insects, the fishes' food, may no longer be able to live in water with a low pH.

Acid rain is a worldwide problem because it can be carried in the atmosphere for great distances before falling back to earth. Pollution sources in midwestern states can actually harm waters on the east coast! As a result, thousands of lakes in the United States, Canada, and other countries are suffering from its effects. If steps are not taken to reduce acid rain, many more bodies of water may be ruined forever.

times more acidic than a pH of 7. A pH of 5 is *100* times more acidic than a pH of 7 and a pH of 4 is *1,000* times more acidic than a pH of 7.

Because carbon dioxide and water found naturally in the atmosphere have a pH of 5.0 to 5.6., natural rain is slightly acidic. However, acid rain that falls in the northeastern United States often ranges from 4.0 to 4.6 pH. In most regions of the country the lakes and rivers can tolerate this acidity without any loss of water quality. A natural buffering ability present in most soils that contain limestone can neutralize acidity. However, several regions of the country are damaged by acid rain because they have thin soils and granite bedrock. Granite is low in limestone and cannot neutralize (buffer) acid precipitation.

The northeast, the Rocky Mountains, areas of the northcentral and southeastern U.S. and eastern Canada are most affected by acid rain.

How You Can Help Reduce Acid Rain:
- Car pool whenever possible.
- Make sure all vehicles at home have their engines tuned properly.
- Conserve electrical use in the home. Oil and phosphate fuels are used at many power plants and contribute to acid rain.

Sewage

Sewage consists of human wastes and garbage. It also includes water used for laundering or bathing. Most sewage is treated at a treatment plant that removes the solids and dissolved substances. However, when a treatment plant gets overloaded or has a malfunction, sewage gets dumped into rivers. Today's laws are quite strict, but sewage pollution is still a major problem, especially in large cities.

Sewage depletes the dissolved

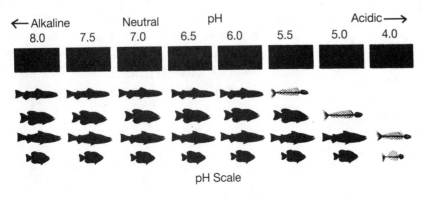
pH Scale

oxygen in water. Sewage wastes contain nutrients that serve as fertilizers. They cause algae (tiny plants) to bloom in great quantities. When these organisms die, oxygen is used for the process of decomposition, and the fish go without adequate oxygen and sometimes die. If this situation gets bad enough, all the fish in a river below a treatment plant may die. As you have learned, fish must have an adequate supply of oxygen or they will not survive.

Raw sewage can also cause serious diseases in humans who use the water or eat shellfish from polluted areas. Sewage may also make waters unhealthy to swim in.

What You Can Do:
- Don't make sewage treatment harder by dumping chemical or other cleansing agents in drains or in the toilet.
- If your house is on a septic system instead of a city sewer system, it is important to service the system periodically.

Industrial Waste

Industries produce everything from food products to hazardous wastes. Most industries produce some form of liquid waste that has to be treated before it is released into public waters. These waste waters contain many toxic chemicals. Although some discharges are treated, some of this chemical waste is still discharged directly into aquatic systems.

What You Can Do To Reduce Industrial Waste:
- Recycle. Some industrial waste can be reduced by recycling.
- Write your legislator and congressional representative. Express the importance of having strong legislation to protect our water resources.
- Never pour anything into a storm drain. Household chemicals, paints, or soaps dumped down the gutter flow into streams untreated.

Petroleum Products

Accidental oil spills can have disastrous effects on aquatic life. Petroleum products can kill by direct contact with the fish's gills. Oil may also suffocate eggs and young fish, since the young inhabit shallow waters where oil tends to concentrate. Marine birds, sea otters and turtles may also be killed.

What You Can Do To Reduce Petroleum Wastes:
- Recycle used automotive oil. Oil drained from cars and disposed of improperly creates more oil in our waters than a single oil spill from a tanker. Drain the oil from your car into a container and take it down to a service station that recycles oil.

Trash

We have become a throw-away society and are running out of dumps to put our trash. Some people do not even try to dispose of their trash appropriately and throw it along our waters. No one enjoys fishing or swimming and having to contend with broken bottles, sharp cans and other trash. Sinking cans, bottles or other trash in the water may put them out of sight temporarily, but they are still there and it is still wrong.

Plastics are particularly hazardous. They are not easily biodegradable and will be around for a long time, maybe for hundreds of years. Thousands of fish and birds die every year from entanglement in plastic six-pack rings that come from canned drinks. Nylon fishing line discarded by thoughtless anglers can also kill birds by entanglement. Some sea turtles even mistake plastic bags for jellyfish (their favorite food) and choke to death when they eat a plastic bag by mistake.

What You Can Do To Reduce Trash:

- Recycle! Always dispose of your trash properly, expecially plastics. If you see trash around your favorite fishing spot, pick it up for recycling or place it in a garbage can where it belongs. Carry a litter bag at all times.
- If you see your friends littering, explain to them that they may be doing a lot more harm than they realize. Don't let them sink cans, bottles or other trash. Even though it goes out of sight temporarily it can cause long-term problems.
- Cut up large tangles of fishing line into short sections before you discard it in a trash can, or recycle it. Some places collect fishing line for recycling. Also cut up six-pack plastic rings. This little extra effort will help save fish, birds and other aquatic animals and will probably make you feel good too.

Nuisance Species

Nuisance species are living organisms that upset the delicate balance of a particular body of water. These may be considered biological pollutants.

Not all bodies of water are the same. Even lakes close together may have different characteristics. In some bodies of water a particular type of fish may be part of the balance. However, in a different body of water that same species may throw off the entire balance. The same is true of some types of vegetation and other aquatic life. Some types of vegetation may prove helpful in one lake and a disaster in another.

For example, crappie are excellent sport fish and in many lakes they fit in well with the balance of the lake. However, if put into a different setting the crappie could ruin the entire lake. In the wrong setting the crappie could populate faster and compete for food and space. You could end up with a lot of little crappie and little else.

Certain kinds of vegetation might be healthy for some water systems. In others, that same vegetation/weed might take over. Too much vegetation can interfere with boating access and protect too many small fish that will then cause an overpopulation of small fish. Also, when weeds die, they decompose removing oxygen from the water. When the oxygen level gets too low, fish will die.

The Great Lakes have had many problems with unwanted species. One problem species introduced by way of ballast water from a ship, was the zebra mussel. The mussel reproduces rapidly. Biologically it is still not known what impact the mussel will have, but it could block spawning grounds for several native fish. The mussel also attaches itself to intakes of water supplies and power plants, causing millions of dollars in damages.

What You Can Do To Prevent Nuisance Species:

- Never release fish from one body of water into another.
- Never release fish or vegetation from an aquarium.
- Never dump your left-over minnows into a lake or river.
- Remove aquatic weeds from trailers and boats and discard them before moving to another lake.

POLLUTION MUST BE STOPPED

Major sources of pollution must be stopped if quality fisheries are to exist. Even the large oceans and estuaries of the world are fragile ecosystems that require attention and careful use to protect them for our future use and enjoyment.

How will you feel if you go fishing and your favorite river is so polluted that the fish have died?

We can all help. While many of these problems seem out of your hands, there are many problems you can solve in your area by getting your classmates, friends, and neighbors to vocally protest the problem.

Our own actions on a daily basis are important. We each have a responsibility to make sure our own actions are not depleting or polluting the water. An individual action, either positive or negative may seem small. However, when you multiply that by millions of us who live in each state, these actions have a tremendous cumulative impact. Remember we all live downstream of someone.

ACTIVITIES

ACTIVITY 1 — TESTING pH

Acid rain can cause severe problems in some areas, but if the soil surrounding the lake contains limestone, the acid can be neutralized.

Limestone is made of calcium carbonate, which is also a major ingredient in antacid tablets. Get two antacid tablets, and crush them into a fine powder.

Get a lemon and squeeze the juice into a glass. The pH of the lemon juice is comparable to the pH of acid rain. Test the juice with litmus paper to determine the pH.

Pour the crushed antacid tablets into the lemon juice and observe the reaction. The acid is being neutralized like soil containing limestone. Now test with litmus paper again to test the pH.

ACTIVITY 2 — HOW MUDDY IS MUDDY?

Pour about 1/4 cup of pond water on a white paper plate. Gently lay a piece of absorbent paper toweling over it to soak up the water. When the toweling is wet, remove it. What is left on the white plate is the sediment or particles of soil that were suspended in the water. However, some may have been picked up on the towel. Take a couple of samples from several ponds and compare them.

ACTIVITY 3 — POLLUTING A POND

To a gallon jar of pond water add some plant fertilizer or even a big shake of fish food. Let your water sit for several days and then observe what is happening. First smell. Then look for green growth, which will indicate rapid algae growth. The oxygen content of this water will drop quickly and fish and other life will die.

ACTIVITY 4 — DEVELOPING A LITTER POSTER

Pollution can be many things. Collect litter from the lake, pond, or area around the pond where you fish. Classify the litter as to composition: paper, plastics, metal, etc.

Construct a poster that depicts the types and amounts of litter you found. Devise a way to help cut down on littering in the area.

ACTIVITY 5 — HOW SILT DESTROYS WATER QUALITY

To show how silt and sediment cover a lake bed or river bottom, make a jar aquarium with gravel and small plastic plants on the bottom. Add clean water. To demonstrate the settlement of silt, take a small jar of dirt and water. Add this mixture to the aquarium and record the results over a period of time. What happens to the dirt in the water? What happens if more dirt is added?

CHAPTER
9
What is a Fish?

All fish are aquatic. This means that although some fish can spend time out of water, all fish must return to water to breathe and to keep from drying out. However, not all creatures that live in water are fish. So, what is a fish?

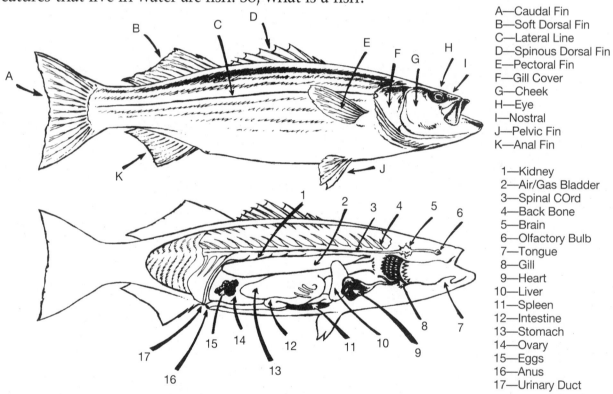

A—Caudal Fin
B—Soft Dorsal Fin
C—Lateral Line
D—Spinous Dorsal Fin
E—Pectoral Fin
F—Gill Cover
G—Cheek
H—Eye
I—Nostral
J—Pelvic Fin
K—Anal Fin

1—Kidney
2—Air/Gas Bladder
3—Spinal COrd
4—Back Bone
5—Brain
6—Olfactory Bulb
7—Tongue
8—Gill
9—Heart
10—Liver
11—Spleen
12—Intestine
13—Stomach
14—Ovary
15—Eggs
16—Anus
17—Urinary Duct

• **Fish are cold-blooded animals.** Cold-blooded means they have a body temperature that is close to that of the water in which they live.
• Fish are the only **vertebrates** (animals with a backbone) **that are able to live in water without breathing air from the atmosphere.**
• Their bodies are supported by a **skeleton**, made up of bone or cartilage, and have a brain case (cranium) that holds the brain.
• **Fish also have permanent gills.** Most fish also have fins, scales, a slimy mucus and a swim bladder.

Fish have been around for more than 400 million years. Today there are about 21,000 species! Fish live in water from a few inches deep to as much as five miles beneath the surface. Fish live in waters from the North and South Poles to the Equator.

Fish come in many sizes, shapes, and colors. Different species (types) prefer different aquatic environments (surroundings) and live their lives in different ways. The more you know about fish, the better the angler you'll become.

PARTS OF A TYPICAL FISH

Fins

Why do fish have fins? Fins make it possible for a fish to stay upright, move and maneuver in water. Fins are thin membranes usually supported by rays or sharp bony spines.

What kinds of fins do fish have and what are their names?

The **dorsal** fin and the **anal** fin help fish keep their balance and move in tight places. **Pectoral** fins are found on each side of a fish's body, just behind its gills, and help a fish stay in one place and to dive or surface. The **pelvic** fins are found on each side of the belly and aid in positioning and balance. The **caudal** fin is another name for the tail fin and it helps fish move.

Some fish, such as salmon, trout, and catfish also have a small, fleshy **adipose** fin on their backs behind the dorsal fin.

Gills

Why do fish have gills? Fish get the oxygen they need to live from water. They use the gills on each side of their head to remove oxygen from the water as it enters through their mouth and then passes over the gills. The gills provide oxygen for life, and without them fish could not live. **Injury to the gills is often fatal.**

Scales

The bodies of most fish are covered with scales. Scales help protect their body from injury and disease. Fish don't grow more scales as they get older, the scales just get bigger. As a fish grows, each scale grows rings like the rings on a cross-

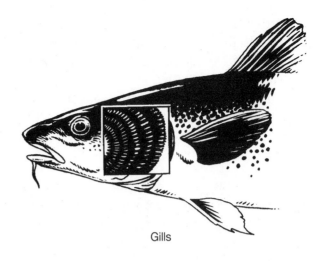
Gills

Rings of Fish Scale

section of a tree trunk. By studying a single scale's rings, scientists can tell a fish's age.

Mucus

Fish are coated by mucus (slime) that helps protect a fish from infection and disease and reduces friction with the water, making it easier to swim. When you plan to release a fish, it's important not to damage this slimy coating. Touching a fishes body can destroy or remove this protective layer. **If you must handle a fish's body, wet your hands first.**

Swim Bladder

Many fish have a gas, or swim, bladder in their bodies. This makes it possible for them to suspend themselves in water and not sink to the bottom. In most fish, the bladder is an air-tight sac; in others fish can add or release gas to remain in deep or shallow water.

Some fish don't have a swim bladder or don't rely on one because they're always moving. Some examples are mackerels, sharks, and tunas.

Skeleton

Most fish have a bony skeleton. However, some fish, including lamprey, sturgeons, and sharks, have skeletons of cartilage rather than bone. The skeleton protects their organs and supports the muscles. The location and flexibility of the spine allow fish to swim.

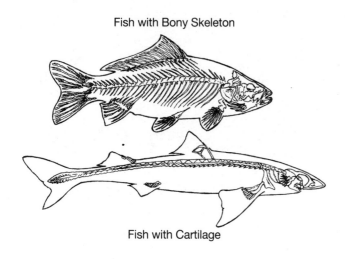

Fish with Bony Skeleton

Fish with Cartilage

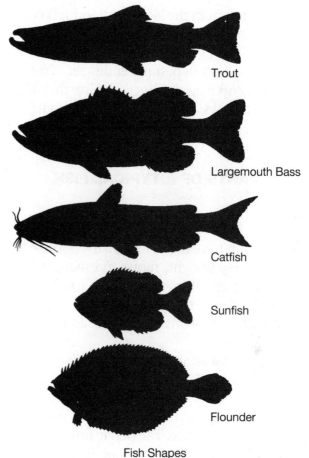

Trout

Largemouth Bass

Catfish

Sunfish

Flounder

Fish Shapes

Flat fish such as flounder often lie right on the bottom. To help them see, both eyes are on one side of their head! Catfish have a body, head shape, and coloration that hint that they live and feed on the bottom. Bluegills are compressed, which indicates that they can move in tight places and do not have great speed.

THE SHAPE OF FISH

Fish come in many shapes. Some are long and narrow. Some are short and thick. The shape of a fish's body gives you a hint as to the way it lives.

For example, a trout that spends most of its life in a river's flowing water has a more streamlined body than a largemouth bass that lives among the weeds in the still waters of a pond or lake. The trout's body is sleek so that flowing water passes around it easily. A bass has a chunkier body and a broad, flat tail that makes the fish highly maneuverable in dense weeds.

FISH COLOR

Fish, especially saltwater fish, come in a variety of colors and patterns. In most cases, the coloring of fish allows them to blend in with the place where they live. For example, the upper part of the body of a bullhead, which spends much of its time near the bottom, is dark. So, from above, it's difficult to see a bullhead against the muddy bottom of a river or a lake.

Pike look like sunlight beaming through a weedbed. Almost every fish is light on its belly and dark on its back. This protective coloring helps them to stay hidden from the smaller fish they feed on, and from larger fish that want to eat them!

HOW FISH SWIM

Most fish swim by moving their bodies in a series of wavy, snake-like motions. Each motion ends with a snap of the tail.

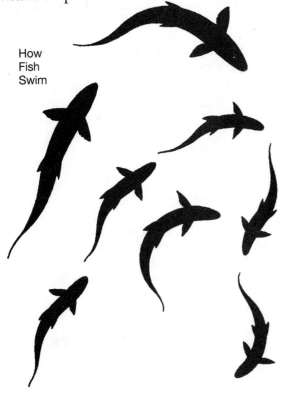

How Fish Swim

Some fish can swim very fast. For example, members of the tuna family can swim up to 50 miles an hour by snapping their tails as much as 10 to 20 times a second! Each tail snap moves a tuna about the length of its body.

THE SENSES OF FISH

Understanding how a fish hears, sees, and smells will help you catch more fish.

How Fish Hear

Fish hear sounds very well and sound travels five times faster in water than it does in air! That's why you hear anglers talk about the need to move quietly on the bank of a pond or in a boat. Fish can be scared away from where you are trying to fish.

How do fish hear? They have "ears" beneath the skin on each side of their heads. Sound reaches the ears through their skin, flesh, and bone.

Fish also have another way to "hear" sounds. It is called the **lateral line**. This line begins at the head and extends almost to the tail along each side of the fish. The lateral line detects any vibrations in the water. This helps them stay in tight schools, navigate streams, detect predators, and find food.

How Fish Smell

The sense of smell is important for many fish. Fish use smell to find food, get warnings of danger, and find their way to spawning areas over long distances. Anadromous fish such as salmon are good examples of this as they can travel several hundred miles to return to their spawning grounds.

All fish have at least two nostrils, called "nares," in their snouts. Behind the nares is a chamber lined with sensors that can detect the slightest odor.

How Fish See

Fish first use their sense of smell or hearing to find food. Many fish then use their sight to make the final attack. Fish can't blink because they have no

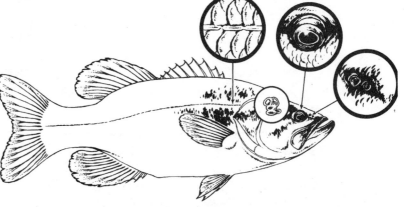

Fish Senses

eyelids. And because they have a fixed iris, they have to move into the shade or into deeper waters to escape bright sunlight. The eyes of fish are round and located on the side of the head.

Fish are also nearsighted! Objects at short distances can be seen very clearly, but objects farther away are blurry. But, they can see nearly all around except for a small area directly behind them.

Can fish can see colors? Scientists say they can. Many species of fish can see at least 24 different shades of color.

Why Fish Senses Are Important

Most fish are alert to what is happening around them. Therefore, once you know how fish use their senses, you will become a better angler.

When an angler sees a fish under water, the fish is actually closer than it seems. This is because light rays bend (refract) as they pass from the air into the water, like light going through a prism. To a fish, an angler standing on the shore seems to be directly over the fish. Because fish can see you on the bank it is important to keep a low profile while fishing.

When trying to approach fish, remember that fish see and hear very well. These factors can determine what you catch. Approach your fishing area quietly and without being seen. Fish can be frightened and leave the area if they see you or if you make lots of noise.

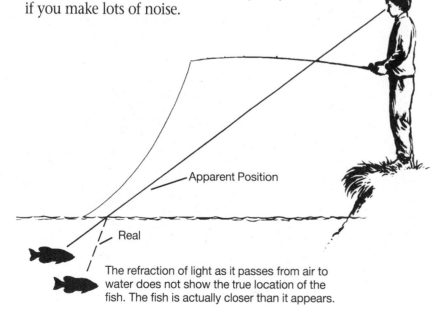

Apparent Position

Real

The refraction of light as it passes from air to water does not show the true location of the fish. The fish is actually closer than it appears.

ACTIVITIES

ACTIVITY 1 — HOW OLD IS YOUR FISH?

For this activity your will need two or more fish of different sizes, tweezers or forceps, and a magnifying glass.

Using the tweezers, carefully pull out a scale. Repeat from the same area on another fish. Compare the size of the scales since they grow as the fish grows. Then examine each with the magnifying glass. Note the "rings" in each. Count the rings to determine each fish's age. Which fish is older? Annual growth shows up as a new ring.

ACTIVITY 2 — IDENTIFYING THE EXTERNAL PARTS OF A FISH

One of the best places to observe healthy, active fish is in an aquarium. If you don't have an aquarium at home visit your local pet store. Introduce yourself to the owner or a worker, and explain why you are there.

By looking at the fish, identify the following:

1. Dorsal fin   5. Caudal fin
2. Anal fin   6. Pelvic fin
3. Pectoral fin   7. Adipose fin
4. Gills   8. Scales

Here are some questions you might ask the owner:

1. How often do you feed them?
2. What do you feed them?
3. Do the fish know when it's feeding time?
4. Why do the tanks have filters?
5. Can the fish see us as we see them?

ACTIVITY 3 — FISH DRAWING

Select your favorite species of fish, draw it and then color. Paste your picture on a piece of poster board or construction paper. On a piece of writing paper, write facts about the fish— the species name, where it lives, what it eats, and what might eat it. After finishing, paste this information under your drawing on the same piece of posterboard.

ACTIVITY 4 — WRITING A FISH STORY

Write a story from a fish's point of view. Tell what kind of fish you are, where you live, how you live, what you eat, and what you hide from.

60

CHAPTER
10
What Kind of Fish is This?

Everyone should know the names of the fish they catch. Studying pictures of fish can help you learn. Seeing live fish is better. Once you have seen a live fish a few times you should at least recognize the family it belongs to. Later, you can try to identify the exact species. For example, after catching a few bass, it will be easy to identify a bass. Later, you will be able to tell whether the fish is a largemouth bass or a smallmouth bass.

How Many Species Of Fish Can You Identify In This Montage?

Fish have two kinds of names. One is a common name. It isn't unusual for the same fish to have many common names, depending on the state where it lives, but a fish has only one scientific name. For example, common names for the largemouth bass include bigmouth bass, black bass, largemouth black bass, green bass, and bayou bass. Its scientific name, however, is always *Micropterus salmoides*, wherever you go.

Most anglers learn to identify fish by sight.

Some fish are easy to identify. Others may be more difficult because some species look alike. To tell the difference between similar species, anglers look closely at the shape, pattern, or color of the fish. Looking at the fins, mouth, and other characteristics will also help tell you what kind of fish it is.

SOME COMMON FRESHWATER FISH

The Sunfish Family

North America has 30 species of fish that are members of the sunfish family. The key to telling them apart is the dorsal fin on the fish's back. All members of this family have a dorsal fin with two connected parts. The front portion has stiff spines while the rear portion has soft rays.

The sunfish family can be separated into three groups-sunfishes, crappies, and the black basses.

The sunfishes include the bluegill, pumpkinseed and longear. The bluegill can be identified by the solid black flap on the gill cover and a dark blotch at the back of the dorsal fin. The pumpkinseed has a bright orange breast and wavy blue bands on its head. The longear has a long black flap on the gill cover with a white margin. The many common names for bluegill will amaze you. In some areas, the bluegill and other sunfish are called bream, roach, sunnies, kivvers, and johnny-roach!

The crappies are the white crappie and the black crappie. Black and white crappies look much alike. Usually, the black crappie has more dark blotches on its body. The white crappie is more silvery with black markings that form seven to nine vertical bars on the sides of its body. To make sure, you can count the spines in the dorsal fin. Black crappies have seven or eight. White crappies have only six.

The black basses include the largemouth, smallmouth, redeye, and spotted bass. To tell the difference between largemouth bass and smallmouth bass, study the jaw. On the largemouth, the jaw extends back beyond the eye. The jaw of the smallmouth, however, extends just behind

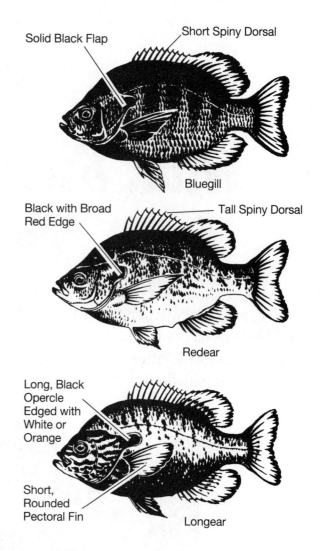

Solid Black Flap   Short Spiny Dorsal

Bluegill

Black with Broad Red Edge   Tall Spiny Dorsal

Redear

Long, Black Opercle Edged with White or Orange

Short, Rounded Pectoral Fin

Longear

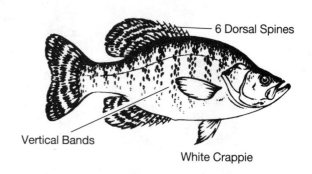

6 Dorsal Spines

Vertical Bands

White Crappie

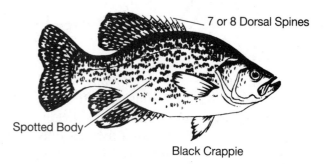

7 or 8 Dorsal Spines

Spotted Body

Black Crappie

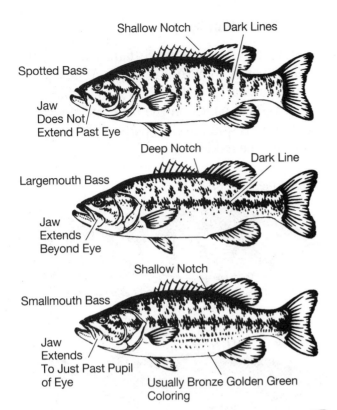

Spotted Bass — Shallow Notch — Dark Lines — Jaw Does Not Extend Past Eye

Largemouth Bass — Deep Notch — Dark Line — Jaw Extends Beyond Eye

Smallmouth Bass — Shallow Notch — Jaw Extends To Just Past Pupil of Eye — Usually Bronze Golden Green Coloring

while chars have lighter spots on a darker background. Cutthroat trout, common in the western states are identified by a red slash mark under the lower jaw.

Chars—The chars include brook trout, lake trout, and Dolly Varden and bull trout. The brook trout has worm like markings on its back and pink or reddish fins edged with white. Dolly Vardens have red, orange, or yellow spots. Lake trout have very pale spots on the body and on the dorsal fin, anal fin, and the tail.

Pacific Salmon—Pacific salmon include the chinook, chum, sockeye, pink, coho, and the steelhead/rainbow trout. The chinook is also called the king salmon and the coho is also called the silver salmon. These fish are found from California to Alaska. In addition, they have been stocked in the Great Lakes and in some other large, freshwater lakes and reservoirs. The rain-

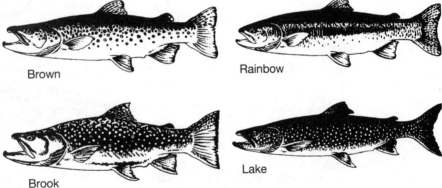

Brown

Rainbow

Brook

Lake

the pupil of the eye. Another way to tell the difference is to look at the dorsal fin. Smallmouth bass have a shallow notch between the spiny and soft-rayed sections. Largemouth have a sharp notch at this same place.

Trout and Salmon

Trout and salmon belong to a family of fish known as the Salmonidae. There are 39 different North American species in the Salmonidae family and all have a fleshy adipose fin between the dorsal fin and the tail.

Scientists break down the family Salmonidae into several groups. The major groups of interest to the angler include trouts, chars, Pacific salmon, grayling and whitefish.

Trouts—The true trouts includes the brown trout, golden trout, cutthroat trout, Apache trout, Gila trout, and Atlantic Salmon. Generally true trouts have darker spots on a lighter background,

bow trout is also stocked in coldwater lakes, rivers and streams throughout North America.

Pacific salmon are **anadromous** fish. This means they live in saltwater but move into freshwater streams and rivers to spawn (lay and

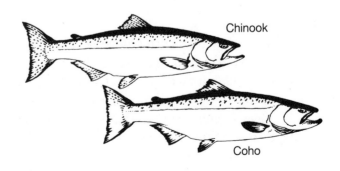

Chinook

Coho

fertilize the eggs). Depending on the time spent in a river, their body color changes from bright silver to dark or brilliant hues.

Whitefish and Grayling—Within the lower 48 states, the whitefishes and grayling live in a limited area in the northern and western states. They are widely distributed in Alaska and Canada.

The Catfish Family

Catfish have smooth skin with no scales. Catfish, however, have "whiskers" or barbels around their mouths that contain many taste buds. Catfish can actually taste their food before they put it into their mouth. Catfish have sharp spines on the dorsal and pectoral fins. If one of these spines punctures your skin, it can cause a painful wound.

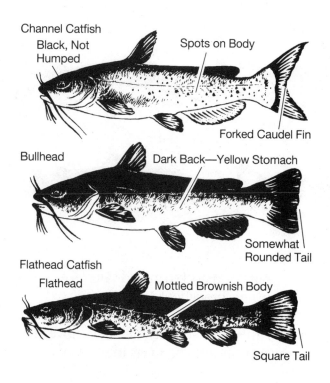

Channel Catfish
Black, Not Humped
Spots on Body
Forked Caudel Fin

Bullhead
Dark Back—Yellow Stomach
Somewhat Rounded Tail

Flathead Catfish
Flathead
Mottled Brownish Body
Square Tail

Bullheads, which are members of the catfish family, have rounded tails, while channel and blue catfish have forked tails. The flathead catfish has an almost square tail, similar in appearance to bullheads. Members of the catfish family also have a large adipose fin between the dorsal fin and the tail.

The Perch Family

The members of the perch family include the yellow perch, walleye, and sauger. Yellow perch have dark backs, yellowish to golden sides, and dark vertical bands on the back and sides. The dorsal fin is split into two parts, and their lower fins may be reddish or orange.

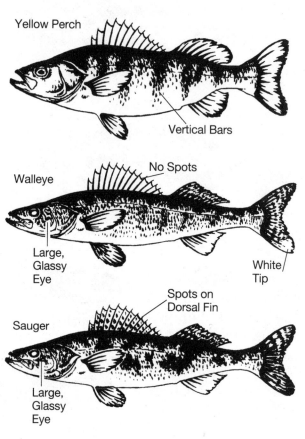

Yellow Perch
Vertical Bars

Walleye
No Spots
Large, Glassy Eye
White Tip

Sauger
Spots on Dorsal Fin
Large, Glassy Eye

Walleye and sauger are difficult to tell apart. Their bodies are round and they have slightly forked tails. You can tell them apart by looking at the spiny dorsal fin. The walleye has a large dark blotch near the base of the last few spines and dark streaks throughout the dorsal fin. The sauger has distinct dark spots throughout the dorsal fin, but no blotch.

They both have sharp teeth and large, glassy eyes. These features allow them to feed on fish, even in the dark! Their bodies are olive-green to golden on the sides and their bellies are white. The tail of a walleye has a silver or white tip. The sauger doesn't have this feature.

The Pike Family

This family includes the chain pickerel, grass pickerel, red fin pickerel, northern pike, and muskellunge (muskie). The members of the pike family have long, slim bodies with the dorsal fin set well back on the body near a forked tail. All pike have long snouts (almost like a duck bill) and sharp teeth. The chain pickerel, which grows to nine pounds, is larger than the grass pickerel or red fin pickerel. It has black, chain-like marking on the sides.

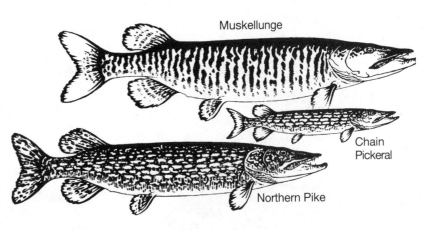

Muskellunge

Chain Pickeral

Northern Pike

The northern pike has bean-shaped spots on its side and dark spots on fins and the tail. The muskellunge has vertical bars on its body. On the northern pike, the entire cheek has scales but only the upper half of the gill has scales. Both the cheek and gill cover are fully scaled on a pickerel. If you look under the jaws of both fish, there are tiny holes. The pike has five on each side. The muskie has six to nine on each side. Pike grow to 50 pounds while muskie may reach 60 pounds!

the striped marlin is higher than that on the blue. Also, the blue marlin has a much higher anal fin than the striped marlin. White marlin have a rounded dorsal fin.

The swordfish has a very long, wide bill and a high, curved dorsal fin.

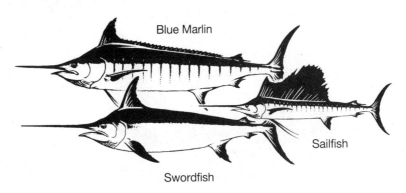

Blue Marlin

Sailfish

Swordfish

SOME COMMON SALTWATER FISH

Billfish

This is the name given to a group of large fish that live in temperate and tropical waters. They all have long, pointed upper jaws that form a "spear" or a "sword." Billfish include the marlins, sailfish, swordfish, and spearfish. Billfish are easy to identify if you study their fins. The sailfish has a large dorsal fin on its back that is taller than the deepest part of its body.

Blue, striped, and black marlin have pointed dorsal fins, but there are other differences. The black marlin has rigid pectoral fins. They don't fold back as they do on the blue and striped marlins. The pointed front of the dorsal fin on

Flounder

Flounder belong to a group of flatfishes that live on the sandy or muddy bottoms of bays and along the shores of most oceans. They have a dark, mottled coloring on one side of their bodies that helps them hide from predators. The other side is white. These fish swim on their right side. Some have both eyes on the left side of their bodies. Others have both eyes on the right side. This characteristic helps you identify particular species.

Summer Flounder

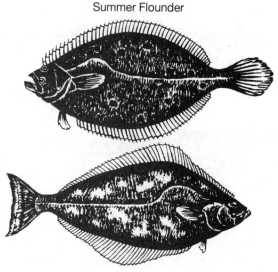

Pacific Halibut

Cods

Members of the cod family are found in cold northern and Arctic waters. Most live in shallow waters near coasts but can be caught in deep water. Almost all cods live on the bottom. They have small scales and soft-rayed fins. Usually, they have a large mouth and a barbel on the chin.

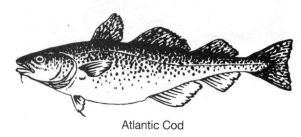

Atlantic Cod

Atlantic Tomcod

Cod family members include the Atlantic cod, tomcod, hake, pollack, and haddock. The only freshwater cod is the burbot. They inhabit cold, deep northern lakes.

The Drum Family

Drums are found throughout the world, generally in temperate and tropical waters. Usually,

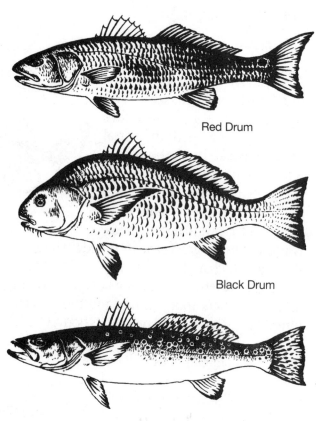

Red Drum

Black Drum

Spotted Sea Trout

they live over sandy bottoms in shallow water near estuaries. They have a lateral line on the sides of the body that extends onto the tail fin. Usually, drums have one or more barbels on the lower jaw.

Members of the drum family include the red drum, black drum, spotted seatrout, common weakfish, corvina, spot, and croakers.

Bluefish

Bluefish range in size from one to over 20 pounds. They are a bright silver and blue color and have powerful jaws lined with sharp teeth. Bluefish eat eels and bait fish that they encounter in their travels.

More anglers pursue bluefish than any other

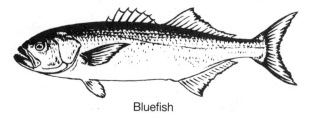

Bluefish

fish on the east coast of the U.S., although their distribution is worldwide. Atlantic Coast fish winter in warm waters off Florida and migrate all the way to Maine by summer's end.

The adults spawn in warmer southern waters. The juveniles (called "snapper blues") head northward just before the adult in the spring. West coast bluefish make similar seasonal migrations along the Pacific Coast.

Rockfish

A variety of species caught along West Coast shores are known collectively as "rockfish." Popular favorites are black rockfish, quillback rockfish, copper rockfish and yelloweye rockfish. Other fish caught in the same areas are greenlings, lingcod, sculpins and dogfish (a shark).

Quillback Rockfish

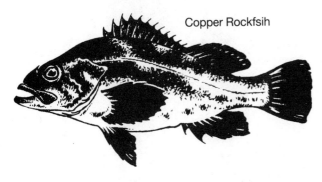

Copper Rockfsih

ANADROMOUS FISH

Anadromous fish are fish that live in saltwater but move into freshwater streams and rivers to spawn. Anadromous fish include fish in a variety of families. They include striped bass, shad, At-

lantic and Pacific salmon, and some sturgeon. Some species of trout and char, including the rainbow or steelhead trout, brown trout, Dolly Varden, brook trout, and cutthroat trout move from freshwater streams and rivers to the ocean or large freshwater lakes for a period of time where they grow at a much faster rate. These are called "sea-run" or "lake-run" fish.

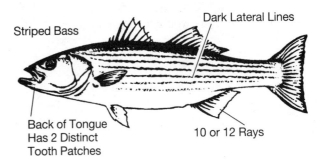

Striped Bass
Dark Lateral Lines
Back of Tongue Has 2 Distinct Tooth Patches
10 or 12 Rays

ACTIVITIES

ACTIVITY 1 — MAKING A FISH PRINT

Using a freshly caught fish, obtain printing ink and rice paper to make a fish print. Carefully roll, paint or spread printing ink onto the fish, covering all parts from head to tail. Using rice paper, slightly longer and wider than your fish, immediately cover the fish while the ink is wet. Pat down gently or rub carefully with a wooden blade over the paper to form your fish ink print. Thin layers of ink produce the best ink print. Remember to hold the paper carefully as you gently rub the paper onto the inked fish. Let your paper dry as you lift it carefully from the fish. Your print can be labeled, autographed, and identifed according to its physical features or simply framed and displayed. Cotton T-shirts work even better than rice paper and can make you a unique shirt!

ACTIVITY 2 — WHO AM I?

Read each of the following phrases and and write the name of the correct fish on the line from the choices provided.

Largemouth Bass, Pumpkinseed, Catfish, Drum, Sunfish, Trout

1. I have whiskers, but don't meow_____
2. I have rays, but not sunbeams _____
3. I have an orange breast, but you can't plant me to grow Jack-0-lanterns _____
4. I sport a wonderful array of colors but no pot of gold _____

5. My jaw goes way beyond my eye, but
   I don't talk much _____

6. I have a lateral line that extends
   into my tail but I'm not musical _____

ACTIVITIY 3 — FISH IDENTIFICATION

Learn to identify fish common to your area. Visit a local bait or sporting goods shop where there are mounted fish on display.

List the names of the fish and ask if they were caught in your area. While looking at the fish, make note of the one thing you think would help you to recognize this species. Compare this trait to other mounts of the same kind and to other types of fish. You will soon find that each species can be easily recognized.

ACTIVITY 4 — MAKING A FISH IDENTIFICATION CHART

Find pictures or draw species of fish that you plan to catch. Make a chart with two columns—one for family of fish and the other for identifying characteristics. Suggestions for fish families include: sunfish, crappie, trout, catfish, perch, pike, billfish, flounder, cod, rockfish, etc.

11

Where Do Fish Live?

To catch fish the angler must first locate them. Fish are found nearly everywhere there is water with enough food, oxygen and cover. Near your home there should be a body of water that has fish living in it.

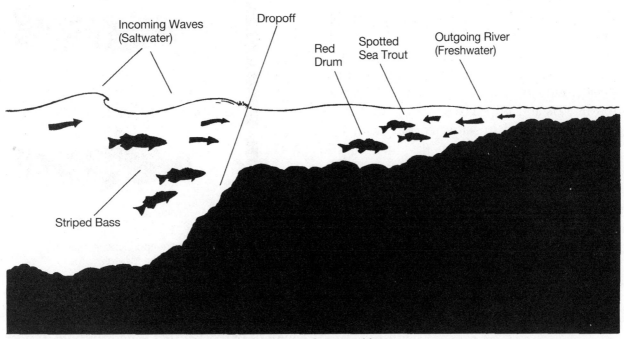

Freshwater & Saltwater Meet

Not all fish can live in the same kind of waters. Fish can tolerate different environmental conditions, including different:

- Amounts of salt
- Amounts of oxygen
- Types and amounts of food
- Water temperature
- Hiding areas (cover and the bottom)
- Breeding areas

SALINITY (AMOUNT OF SALT)

One major factor that separates fish is salt. Some fish cannot live in areas where there is much salt and others need salt in the water to live. However, some fish can live in both saltwater and freshwater!

Freshwater

Freshwater contains much less salt than the ocean. Most ponds, reservoirs, and rivers across

North America are freshwater. Some common freshwater fish are bluegills, carp, catfish, crappie, bass, perch, northern pike, trout, and walleye.

Saltwater

Many kinds of fish live in the salty water of the oceans. A fish's kidney keeps the proper balance of salt in its body. Popular saltwater fish are bluefish, cod, flounder, striped bass (also found in freshwater), sea trout, tarpon, tuna, halibut, rockfish, seaperch, lingcod, and yellowtail.

Brackish Water

An estuary is where fresh water streams and rivers meet the salt water from the ocean. The amount of salt (salinity) changes daily with the flow of tides, rain, or drought. This water is termed "brackish." Changes in the amount of salinity will determine which fish can live in the area. Species found in these waters include redfish, sea trout, snook and striped bass.

Some fish live in saltwater, but swim up streams and rivers to spawn (lay their eggs). These fish are called **anadromous fish.** They include shad, salmon, and some types of trout.

OXYGEN

Without an adequate supply of oxygen in the water, fish cannot survive. Fish such as carp can live on less oxygen than fish like trout. **What can affect the amount of oxygen in the water?** Living plants within a lake or stream add oxygen to the water through **photosynthesis**—the process of using sunlight to make food. Oxygen can also enter water from the surrounding air. In a stream, moving water tumbling over rocks picks up oxygen from the air.

Decaying plants use oxygen from the water to decompose. Pollution of many kinds reduces oxygen in water. Chemicals dumped into water trap oxygen and take it out of the natural system. Thermal pollution, the heating of water through industrial use, reduces the amount of oxygen

MORE

Brook Trout
5 ppm

Largemouth Bass
4 ppm

OXYGEN

Carp
3 ppm

Bullhead
2 ppm

LESS

The oxygen levels listed are approximate minimum requirements (ppm = Parts Per Million).

water can hold. Water temperature affects the amount of oxygen that water can hold. Colder water can hold more oxygen molecules than warm water. Oxygen levels can change from one location to another in the same body of water.

FOOD

The amount and type of food available plays an important role in which fish will be present in a body of water. The amount of competition with other fish is also a factor. This will be covered in greater detail in Chapter 12.

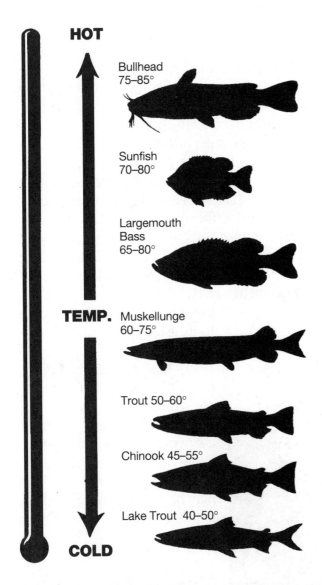

HOT

Bullhead
75–85°

Sunfish
70–80°

Largemouth
Bass
65–80°

TEMP. Muskellunge
60–75°

Trout 50–60°

Chinook 45–55°

Lake Trout 40–50°

COLD

The temperatures shown are optimum ranges. However all of these fish may survive in near freezing water temperatures.

WATER TEMPERATURES

Each fish has a different range of water temperature in which it can survive. Some fish can live in a wide range of temperatures, but trout require cold water. Although fish cannot always find the exact temperature they prefer, they are usually found in water close to that temperature.

WATER QUALITY

Fish must have water with adequate oxygen in which to live. Good-quality water will support more species of fish and greater populations of fish than polluted water. Water that is stagnant, polluted, or lacking adequate oxygen will not support large numbers of fish.

Water quality affects fish species differently. Some fish can live in poorer water conditions than others. For example, carp can live in water that trout could not tolerate.

COVER

Cover such as aquatic plants, rocks, logs, or any other type of cover is a requirement for many fish. Fish choose certain types of cover for two main reasons. First, it provides them with protection from enemies. Second, it puts them in the best possible position from which to catch an unsuspecting meal that is drifting or swimming by.

AQUATIC HABITATS WHERE FISH LIVE

Each species of fish prefers a certain habitat. Habitat is where a fish lives and must contain: adequate oxygen, tolerable temperature, adequate food and hiding places (cover). Suitable spawning habitat must be available for fish to reproduce.

Freshwater Lakes And Ponds

Many lakes were formed thousands of years ago by glaciers, massive "rivers" of ice, which carved valleys and holes into the earth. These valleys and holes were filled with melting water from the glaciers and became lakes. Dams built to block the flow of rivers have also formed lakes, often called reservoirs or impoundments.

Ponds are tiny lakes and many are shaped like a bowl. Many farm ponds are used to store rainwater for crops or livestock. They are often great places to fish!

The Water's Surface. Many tiny creatures live right on the water's surface in lakes and ponds. If you look very closely, you may be able to see these dust-size creatures.

For some fish, the surface is a good place to feed. Bass, bluegill, and trout often eat insects that fall on the water. Anything that makes a disturbance on the water's surface attracts the attention of fish. Small fish swimming near the surface can be an easy meal for larger fish.

Open Water. "Plankton" are tiny plants (phytoplankton) and animals (zooplankton) in the water. Most are smaller than the head of a pin! Small fish like to roam open areas of a lake and feed on zooplankton. Larger fish often follow these small fish and feed on them. Then anglers try to catch the larger fish. This is called a "food chain."

Larger fish usually lurk below the small fish, forcing them toward the surface. Whenever you see small fish on the surface in open water, it usually means that larger fish are feeding. While feeding on these fish, they may make splashes you can see.

Other signs that larger fish are nearby are the frantic movements of the small fish. The small fish may even jump out of the water while trying to escape!

The Shoreline Shallows. The shallow water along the shore (littoral zone) is important. This is where many rooted plants, such as cattails, rushes, lilies, pondweed, and marsh grasses, grow.

Some lakes also have areas covered by rootless floating plants that make it difficult to fish. All of these plants are important because they produce the oxygen that fish need to live. They also provide a place for fish to find food and shelter from other hungry fish.

Shallow water attracts both small and large fish. Small fish, like bluegill, spawn, feed and hide in the plants, brush-piles, and logs in the shoreline shallows. Larger fish come to the shallows to feed on the smaller fish and also to spawn. Northern pike and bass often hide in the weeds and ambush smaller fish as they swim by. Larger fish often come to the shallows when there isn't much light. That's why early morning and evening are some of the best times to fish shallow areas.

Deep Water. Deep water is a home for many types of aquatic life. There is little light, no current, and the water temperature changes less than at the surface. Deep water is a good place for aquatic animals to hide, but there may be too little oxygen to sustain life, especially in late summer.

Freshwater Rivers And Streams

Flowing rivers and streams are always changing. Water currents constantly carry sediment (sand, rock and soil) downstream. The shape of a river bed controls the amount of water and sediment the river can carry.

During or after a heavy rainfall, the water level and the speed of a water current increases. This enables the river to carry suspended sediments and results in the "murky" or muddy water you often see.

The water level in a river can drop quickly in very dry weather. During a drought a river can be reduced to a series of pools. This forces fish and other creatures to adjust to the new conditions if they are to live.

72

Fish Locations in Flowing Water

The River Banks. In a straight stretch of river, the main force of the current is in the middle. The deepest water is also in the middle and the area near the shore is the shallowest. When there's a sharp bend in the river, however, the strongest current and deepest water is at the outside edge of the bend.

Deep Water. In flowing water, there is less current near the bottom. Because of this, most fish stay with their bellies almost touching the bottom. They like to take advantage of low spots and other structure that have even less current than the surrounding water. They do this to save their energy and to avoid being pushed downstream.

Most fish in a river face the flow of water and wait for food to come to them. Trout and salmon like cold, moving water. Usually, they'll stay near the edge of the current and eat whatever food comes along. At night or when light levels are low, the fish often move to shallow water to feed.

Estuaries

An estuary is the wide lower course of a river where the river's current meets the tides. In most estuaries this is where salty water mixes with the fresh water of rivers or streams. An ocean tide brings in saltwater and carries out some freshwater. As the waters mix, the water with the most salt is near the bottom. The water with less salt, called "brackish" water, is near the surface because it is lighter.

An estuary is exciting for anglers because both freshwater and saltwater species of fish live there. Estuaries are biologically very productive areas, but they are often converted to industrial sites.

Wetlands

A wetland is an area of wet, spongy land where the water remains near or above the surface of the ground for most of the year. Wetlands are often found between open water and dry land. There are several types of wetlands including marshes, swamps and bogs. Wetlands occur in freshwater, saltwater and estuaries. Almost all are teeming with life.

Many people used to think that wetlands were waste areas. For this reason more than 50% of the wetlands in our country have been drained or destroyed. What a mistake!

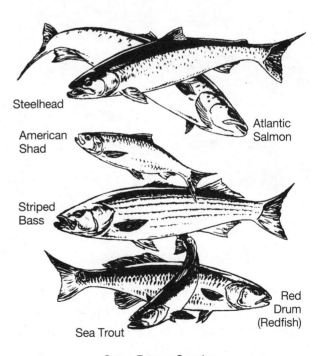

Steelhead

American Shad

Atlantic Salmon

Striped Bass

Sea Trout

Red Drum (Redfish)

Some Estuary Species

Today we understand that wetlands provide vital spawning habitat for numerous fish, and are also important to birds and mammals.

Wetlands are also important because they help to purify our water by filtering out impurities and sediment. Wetlands also help control floods and store large amounts of water for a long time.

Marshes and swamps are very important areas for fish. Marshes are more open and have grasses, reeds and other non-woody plants. Swamps have many trees and shrubs.

Most **bogs** are found in northern climates. Bogs are areas with acidic soil and a heavy growth of mosses. Peat moss is formed in bogs by the build up and partial decay of plants. Because of the acid water, fish are usually not found in bogs.

RIPARIAN ZONES

Riparian areas are a middle zone of vegetation along streams and rivers. Due to the influence of water, the vegetation in a riparian zone is typically larger and more dense than the vegetation outside the zone.

In the drier parts of the country, riparian zones are very obvious. Only the small section near the water has any green vegetation. In parts of the country where more rainfall occurs, riparian zones are not as easy to point out, but they do exist.

Like wetlands, quality riparian areas play a vital role in maintaining the quality of the water in streams and rivers. When humans or livestock destroy the vegetation, the quality of the water is not as good.

Riparian vegetation provides food and shade for aquatic plants and animals. Leaf litter and terrestrial insects fall from vegetation into streams, providing a source of food for fish. Elimination of the vegetation along the river can cause the temperature of the river to rise because there is nothing to shade the water from the sun.

Quality riparian zones can cleanse water and act as a sponge in times of heavy rain. This assists in the prevention of flooding. When the rains stop, and water levels drop in the river, the riparian area slowly releases water back into the river. This helps the river or stream to maintain a more stable water supply for fish and other plants and animals that depend on it.

Riparian Zone

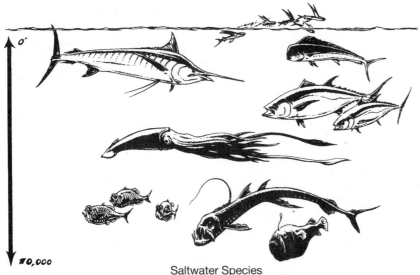

0'

10,000

Saltwater Species

THE OCEANS

Did you know that land takes up only one quarter of the earth? Oceans cover nearly three-fourths of the Earth's surface!

The Intertidal Zone

The intertidal zone is a low, flat area of the shore. It is the area covered by the sea at high tide and exposed at low tide. Crabs, snails and other creatures live here. Predator fish, like sharks, feed in this shallow area at high tide. Their bellies may scrape the bottom while their fins and backs are out of the water. Many other kinds of fish also feed in this zone because it is rich in food. On the West Coast tides can fluctuate 15 to 20 feet. Almost all bank fishing is done in this environment.

Coastal Waters

Coastal or waters near shore, are seldom as clear as the open ocean. Lots of sediments are stirred up by waves. Water temperature affects the variety of creatures in the water. The warmer coastal water has more forms of life than the colder waters of the open ocean.

In coastal areas, the ocean bottom may have sections of exposed rock, but most of it is sand or sediment. Fish live at all depths in this coastal water. Most, however, are found close to the bottom. Many feed near cover such as a rock or a coral reef where they can ambush prey. Other fish roam, searching for an easy meal.

Most saltwater anglers fish in coastal waters, because there are dozens of different fish species to choose from. Many marine fish migrate up and down the coastline seasonally. Smart anglers monitor water temperatures to determine which species they should be fishing for.

The Open Ocean

Most kinds of fish that live offshore grow quickly, at least during their early years. A marlin grows from the size of a pinhead to 9-1/2 pounds in 12 weeks! Catching large fish in the open ocean takes special tackle, great skill, stamina, and large, safe boats.

ACTIVITIES

ACTIVITY 1 — HABITAT SCRAMBLE
See if you can figure out the water habitats or fish by using the clue to unscramble the word. Write the answers, from the choices below, on the line provided.

Estuaries, shoreline shallows, bogs, oceans, ponds, lakes, intertidal zone, rivers, wetlands, coastal waters

1. dsonp. . . . . . tiny lakes _____
2. wleatnds. . . . . wet, spongy land _____
3. lisoheiren hslaslwo. . . . rooted plants live here (2 words) _____ _____
4. errvis. . . . . . cause erosion _____
5. sgbo . . . . . . soggy, acidic areas _____
6. sacltoa tswear . . . have a mostly sandy or sediment bottom (2 words) _____ _____
7. dtinlaetri eozn. . .uncovered at low tide (2 words)_____ _____
8. eansco . . . . . covers 3/4 of the earth's surface_____
9. risseetau . . . . salt and freshwater mix _____
10. klase . . . . . carved by glaciers _____

ACTIVITY 2 — HOW WATER TEMPERATURE AFFECTS OXYGEN LEVELS IN WATER

For this activity you will need the following: 1 goldfish, a thermometer, and a clear container (gallon jar).

Place a large goldfish in water that is room-temperature. Observe the movement of the gill covers. Count the gill movements (gulps) for 30 seconds. Do this five times, and figure the average number of gulps per session.

Now pour some warm water from your hot water tap into the water. (Use enough warm water so that the temperature increase is noticeable—about 5 degrees F). Wait about 10 minutes, repeat your observations, compute the average number of times the fish gulps per session, and compare the two averages.

When did the fish gulp more, in warm or in cold water? The fish gulps more when there is less oxygen: he is gulping more to get more.

Hopefully, this activity will show you that cold water can hold more oxygen than warm water.

ACTIVITY — 3: ECOSYSTEM WORDSEARCH

This wordsearch has 15 words that can be classified as Animal, Plant, or Nonliving. Divide a paper into three columns labeled with these three classifications. As you find a word, write it in the proper column and circle it in the puzzle. Remember, the words may run in any direction.

ACTIVITY 4 — MAKING A SHOE-BOX ECOSYSTEM

Make a shoe box ecosystem for fish. Show the bottom of a pond or stream—structure, food sources, plants, water level, and fish. Turn the shoe box on its side and add details to make a three-dimensional view. Many can be made from construction paper. Other materials such as stones can represent boulders; sticks can represent dead trees, etc. Use your imagination as you develop your ecosystem.

```
Word Puzzle . . . . . .

W E H S I F T A C W B D H K I L          ALGAE
W L J C F P X T H A N Q E S S O          BREAM
Y J D B T K K L Q R P X R K D M          CATFISH
R A V E W X O N B K S E O Y L J          CATTAIL
J H S I D B R E A M T A N P Z O          DUCKWEED
E T Y X E S H R C A T T A I L A          FISH
R V V N E S S A R G T T T S M T          GRASS
U T J O W X M T A M P O B J S R          HAWK
T S R O K A O H G W O N N I M I          HERON
A R K C C N Q G P C Z U K W A H          MINNOW
R F W A U N C I N N K B R W T X          OAK
E L I R D E K L N A T E O U P G          SUNLIGHT
P U E S H A Y N O P T R V M X E          TEMPERATURE
M B Y Z H G N U Y A M S J T N Y          WATER
E F X S W L Z S W S V F H R J R          WORMS
T V L T I A A L I R B B K H L B
```

CHAPTER
12
What Do Fish Eat?

If you like to fish for bluegill, you may think that all you need to do is learn about bluegill. But to know bluegill you have to know the following things about a bluegill's habitat:

Food Chain

• How is a bluegill affected by non-living things such as water, temperature, pH, and chemicals?

• How is a bluegill affected by living things in the water such as plants, other fish, and other animals that live in the water?

• How is a bluegill affected by living things around the pond such as birds and humans?

• How is a bluegill affected by non-living things that come into water such as soil, pesticides, and trash?

This is what **ecology** is all about. **Ecology is the study of the relationships of organisms with other organisms and non-living factors.** You have learned about non-living factors that affect fish. In this chapter you will learn about the living organisms that relate to the fish. To make this relationship easy to understand, think of the bluegill as part of a food chain or food web.

FOOD CHAINS AND WEBS

All living organisms belong to "food chains." A food chain is made up of a series of organisms that produce and consume food. It is the path that food (materials and energy) takes through a group of organisms.

For example, a food chain may begin with tiny floating plants (phytoplankton) and small animals (zooplankton) that eat the plants. The next step in the chain may be small fish like bluegill that eat the small organisms. The next step may be a largemouth bass that eat bluegills. The final step may be an angler who catches and eats the largemouth bass, or a crayfish that eats the largemouth bass after it has died.

An **ecosystem** is more complex than this example. An ecosystem may have hundreds of food chains intertwined and linked together. Northern pike, for instance, do not exist only on bluegill so pike are part of other food chains, too. Also, other big fish like largemouth bass eat bluegill, so bluegill are part of other food chains. Everything is then a part of a "food web."

Food chains link together to form **food webs**. If you pull any one part of that web, you affect everything in the web. If you take away or pollute the water, the bluegill cannot survive. But what if you take away the plants? The bluegill does not feed on plants, but it feeds on the insects and other organisms that eat the plants. If the plants are gone, then the insects are also gone. Also, if you take away the plants where will the bluegill hide from bigger fish? What will happen to the bigger fish if the bluegill are gone?

To further understand this, it helps to know the different roles played in the food chain. In a lake or an ocean, living organisms are either **producers** of food or they are **consumers**. In some cases, organisms can be both.

Producers

Green plants and algae are producers. They use water and the energy from the sun to produce their own food through a process called photosynthesis. Plants produce oxygen when bathed in sunlight. Green plants use some of the food for themselves. The rest is used by other forms of life. Plants are the basis of all life on earth!

Plants form the broad base of the food chain. Animals could not live without green plants. Rooted plants are extremely visible, but the food chain usually begins with one-celled microscopic organisms. They are almost impossible to see with the naked eye. These plants are called "**phytoplankton.**" **Plankton** is a general term for all of the small life in the water.

Consumers

Animals are consumers. Some animals, called primary consumers or **herbivores**, feed on plant life. Some herbivores are extremely small animals called **zooplankton** that feed on microscopic plants. Other examples of herbivores are insects, worms, shrimp, and some fish.

Carnivores are meat eaters and form the second order of consumers. Some scientists call these animals "foragers." Many panfish such as bluegills and crappie fall into this category along with crayfish, shiners, crabs, alewives, and menhaden.

Predators are even higher level consumers, preying on herbivores and carnivores. These are the gamefish that many anglers want to catch and include pike, muskie, bass, trout, salmon, tuna, tarpon, and bluefish. Some fish's diets change as they grow older. Very young bass may eat algae and microscopic animals at first but switch to insects, smaller fish and other animals as they grow older. Finally, human beings are the highest order consumers, eating organisms from all the levels below them.

Decomposers

Decomposers are things like bacteria and other microbes that break down dead plants and animals. As dead plants and animals decay through this process, they release basic nutrients back into the system. These nutrients are used by plants during photosynthesis and by other animals in their battle for life.

Predators And Prey

Each species of fish relates in a number of ways to other species of fish. Each species relates to others it hunts for food, to others it competes with for food, and to those that it is food for.

At some time in its life, every fish can be considered a predator—a fish that preys on another animal. Bluegill, often the prey of largemouth bass, raid the nests of the bass and eat the eggs. Also, after bass eggs hatch bluegill will eat newly hatched bass fry. Through this reversal of the predator-prey relationship, fish populations are kept in check.

Predator fish try to stay close to their prey. Some lie in ambush until a victim comes close. The prey is captured as the predator bursts from its hiding place. Barracuda, flounder, largemouth bass, muskie, northern pike, and trout often do this. Others search under rocks for food. Tautog (blackfish) searching for crabs or smallmouth bass chasing crayfish are good examples of this. Still other predator fish swim, sometimes in schools, to find prey. Many kinds of saltwater fish such as tuna, bluefish, and mackerel do this.

Predator fish select and attack one victim at a time. They prefer a victim that is alone, injured, or simply looks or behaves differently. That is why many lures are designed to look like an injured minnow. Predator fish also prefer to attack prey from below.

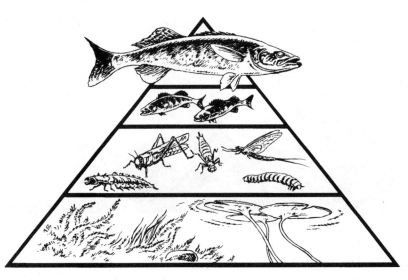

Food Pyramid

Carrying Capacity

Every body of water has a limit on the number of living things it can support. This is called carrying capacity. Food supply plays a vital role in determining the carrying capacity and the size of fish in a particular body of water. Carrying capacity can be shown as a pyramid. For example, large walleye require a great deal of food to survive each fishing season. To produce and sustain a ten-pound walleye requires about 100 pounds of perch each year. One hundred pounds of perch depend on one ton of minnows. These minnows need five tons of worms and insects to survive and the worms and insects need 50 tons of plants for their support. In this example of a pyramid, it takes 50 tons of plants for one ten-pound walleye. Now you can see how valuable one large gamefish is!

USING FOOD-CHAIN INFORMATION IN FISHING

You can be a successful angler if you learn to fish productive water. Look for plant growth, algae, and minnows in the water you fish. Without this food base, the number of predator game fish will be limited. Turn over several rocks or logs on the bank. If you find a crayfish you can almost be

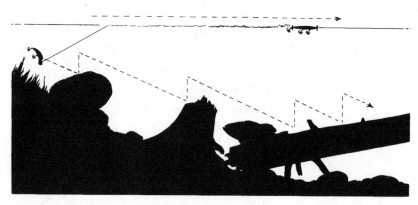

Water that is stagnant and/or polluted with pesticides, chemicals, and trash has few plants. It may not have enough oxygen to support a good fish population. You probably will not have much luck fishing this kind of water.

If you are fishing for predator fish that ambush their prey, you should fish close to places where the fish may be hiding. Work your bait close to tree stumps, weed lines, and open spots in weed beds. Your success will probably increase if you can make your lure appear to be injured. Remember, predators attack one victim at a time and are attracted to those that appear injured.

Through applying your understanding of the food chain you will catch more fish. Learn all that you can about the fish you want to catch! Then, select a productive area to fish, present your lure or bait skillfully, and HOLD ON TO YOUR ROD!!

certain that there will be bass in the lake. Look for living things such as bugs, worms, spiders, dragonflies or other insects that can provide food for fish.

Use Poppers on water surface

Use Jigs for deep fish

Fishing For Bluefish

ACTIVITIES

ACTIVITY 1 — MAKING A MINI-ECOSYSTEM

First you need a gallon glass jar. Your school cafeteria might have an empty one that they would let you have. Make sure that it is completely clean by rinsing thoroughly with hot water. Do not wash with soap or detergent. Fill the jar with fresh water. If you use city tap water you need to let it stand for 24 hours so that chemicals added by water-treatment plants evaporate. Add some elodea or another water plant purchased from a pet store. Finally, add a snail and seal the jar tightly with a lid. Place it in a nice sunny place. The plant (a producer) will provide the oxygen and food for the snail. The snail will provide the carbon dioxide and waste materials for the plant. How many snails do you think could be placed in your jar before it is too crowded or over its carrying capacity?

Fishing For Tautog (Blackfish) Using Crabs in Rocky Habitat

ACTIVITY 2 — MAKING A FOOD WEB

From magazines, collect pictures of a fish, wading bird, frog, minnow, man, eagle, snake, and a water insect. Starting with the frog, lay out the picture on a piece of poster board. Now place the insect picture about two inches away to the right. Very lightly draw an arrow from the insect to the frog. About two inches below the insect place the fish. Now draw an arrow from the insect to the fish, an arrow from the frog to the fish, and one from the fish to the frog. Continue adding pictures and drawing arrows, making sure the arrows point from the animal doing the eating to the one being eaten.

You have produced a food web that can tell you a lot about the relationships between animals. What would happen to the other animals if the insects were to die off? What would happen if the frog population should rise drastically?

ACTIVITY 3 — SEASONAL LURE PREFERENCES OF FISH

Pick a species of fish and find out what lures attract this species. Draw or find pictures of these lures. Make a chart to show the best seasons to use the lures you have selected. Each lure should be written in the column or columns when it is best used.

Type of Fish_____
Good for: Summer Spring Fall Winter

13

Why Do Fish Act The Way They Do?

Learning why fish act the way they do is both interesting and important. Once you understand their behavior, you will appreciate fish and their role in nature. You can then use this information to know where and how to fish.

THE FISH'S BODY

Shape Of The Body

The body shape of a fish controls what it does, how it moves, and what it eats. For example, the northern pike and the barracuda have

long, slender bodies. They are able to lunge ahead quickly to strike at a small fish or a lure. They can't, however, turn as quickly as a bass or a bluegill to catch food or chase your lure or bait.

The shape of their body also controls the speed at which they can swim. Trout and salmon are fast swimmers because their body muscles control wide, powerful tails. Carp, sea bass, and yellow perch are not fast swimmers, but they slowly cover productive areas in search of food. Usually, the larger the fish, the faster it can swim.

Senses

The senses of some fish are better developed than those of others. Some fish use their sense of smell to find food. Eels and salmon are well known for their ability to smell. Other fish, such as bonefish, sturgeon, and catfish, use their sense of taste to feed. Catfish have taste buds all over their bodies so that they can taste food even before taking it into their mouths. Many fish use their senses of sight and hearing to feed. These include barracuda, billfish, striped bass, and trout. Sharks use the senses of sight, sound, and smell to feed.

Shape And Location Of The Mouth

You can also tell where fish like to feed by looking at the shapes and locations of their mouths. The sharp, pointy teeth of fish like the muskellunge, walleye, sea trout, and bluefish make them ideal for catching and holding slippery baitfish. The mouth of fish like the catfish, sturgeon, bonefish, carp, and cod makes them ideal bottom-feeders. Bottom-feeders are constantly moving while other fish prefer to wait and ambush passing food.

HABITAT

Different fish prefer different kinds of living areas, or habitat. Some fish like the open waters of a lake or an ocean. Fish that like open waters are sometimes called "free-swimmers." They swim from place to place searching for food and water that has the most comfortable levels of oxygen, water temperature, and other living conditions. Saltwater free-swimmers include billfish, bluefish, dolphin, and tuna. Freshwater free-swimmers include crappie and perch in lakes and ponds, and coho and chinook salmon in the Great Lakes.

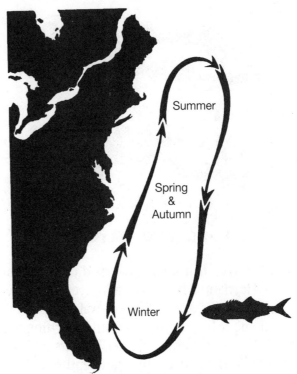

Bluefish Migration

Other fish like to spend much of their time near certain objects or structure in the water. Some saltwater fish prefer nearshore structure such as sand bars, rocky bottoms, and oyster beds. These include sea bass, sea trout, and tautog. Many freshwater fish, including largemouth bass, northern pike, muskellunge, and walleye, also like to spend much of their time near some kind of structure such as a drop-off or near a weed bed.

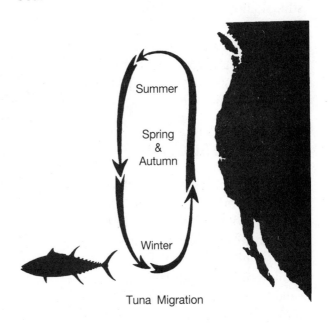

Tuna Migration

Fish Near Structure

FOOD AND OXYGEN

Just like you, fish must have food on a regular basis. How and what a fish eats affects its movement and presence at different water depths.

Some fish feed by constantly searching the bottom (suckers and flounder), others actively feed from the surface, the mid-depths, and on the bottom (bluefish/trout). Some will pick up any type of dead bait (catfish) while others insist on live bait or a lure that resembles live bait (billfish and barracuda).

A fish uses a considerable amount of energy to find food and eat. To save energy, some fish hide and wait for food to come by. Other fish hunt for food constantly.

Fish also need oxygen in the water. Trout live well in swift-flowing streams with plenty of oxygen, while carp and bullheads can survive in still, shallow waters with much less oxygen.

In colder water, a fish needs less oxygen and food. In warmer water, a fish breathes more quickly and feeds more often.

REPRODUCTION

Reproduction, or spawning, plays a very important role in the life and behavior of fish. In spring, largemouth bass, bluegill, crappie, and other fish come into the shallows to make beds, sometimes called nests, for laying eggs. They make these nests using their tails

Atlantic Salmon Migration

to "sweep" the bottom and clear a place for their eggs.

Salmon and shad make long migrations from the ocean to the headwaters of rivers to lay eggs in the same waters where they were hatched. They deposit their eggs in beds that they carve out of the stream bottom. Striped bass and yellow perch make similar, shorter spawning runs up tidal or tributary streams to spawn.

Some fish do not lay their eggs in nests but in open water.

Fish Spawning

Walleye deposit their eggs over gravel bars or rocks, where water flow keeps them from getting covered with silt or dirt. Bluefish and grass carp broadcast their eggs in open water to increase hatching success.

Most fish spawn in spring, but brook and brown trout, most Pacific salmon and lake trout spawn in the fall.

Fish Locations—Summer

Fish Locations—Winter

SEASONS AND MOVE-MENT

Fish react to the changing seasons. During the year, there are changes in water temperature, the amount of light, and the number of hours of daylight. In summer, there is more light and more hours of sunlight than during the winter. When light increases, fish such as flounder and bass, move out of the unprotected shallows (where they could become prey for birds or shore animals) and move to deeper waters. When water temperatures are lower during the winter months in northern areas, the activity of fish slows down. The fish also eat less food and may be found in deeper waters. When water warms in the spring, most fish return to shallower waters, begin spawning, and feed more often. Anglers call this cycle a "seasonal pattern." Species of fish can be counted on to repeat this pattern year after year.

Fishermen use this kind of information to become better anglers.

A saltwater fish's movements are based on season, tides, currents resulting from tidal flows, and movement of their prey. Bluefish found in Florida in the winter may be found in Maine during the following summer. Similarly, tuna "wintering" in Mexico, may visit Canada in the summer!

CURRENT

Fish react to current in different ways. Some fish hide or rest by a rock or other structure. Other fish will seek a current and follow it for the informa-

tion (smell, taste, temperature) that it provides.

In all cases fish will head into a current. This doesn't always mean they will be facing upstream. An eddy is a current, often found below a dam, that turns back upstream. A fish in an eddie will be facing downstream but headed into the eddy current.

It is important for you to learn what affects the behavior of the species you are trying to catch. If you understand them and their life style, you will have a better chance of catching them.

ACTIVITIES

ACTIVITY 1 — VEGGIE FISH

Select several vegetables, such as a carrot, celery, onion, and potato. Assume that each of these is a fish shape. Now fill the sink with water. Move your veggie fish through the water. Watch the ripples and feel how they move through the water. Which one has the most drag or pull? Which glides easily. Which color would give the most protection in a muddy pond? Add fins cut from a cardboard container or a milk carton. Make a cut in your vegetable and insert your fins. Check you manual to make sure you have included all of the fins.

ACTIVITY 2 — CAN FISH HEAR?

Using a fish in a bowl or aquarium, try to determine if it can hear you speak. Try this.

Every day before you feed the fish, yell at it from a distance of about two feet. Yell the fish's name, call it as you would your dog or just yell any word.

After ten days of doing this, see if the fish comes to you or to the area in which you normally put the food.

Try the same experiment again, except this time, tap on the glass instead of yelling. How does the fish react after ten days?

What does this tell you about how fish learn what is going on around them.

ACTIVITY 3 — OBSERVATION OF FISH BEHAVIOR

Visit an aquarium where fish can be observed. Notice: (1) how many times the fish opens and closes its mouth in one minute; (2) how many times the gills of the fish open and close in one minute; (3) how long the fish remains in the same location; (4) how many movements the fish makes in one minute; (5) where the fish remains according to water level (top, middle, and bottom); (6) what behaviors the fish shows when swimming, resting, eating or searching for food. Notice any reaction of the fish to loud noises, or slow or rapid movements of an object in the water moving toward the fish. Identify the kind of fish being observed and its habitat. Write down your observations for future reference.

CHAPTER
14
More Fish For Everyone!

It seems like everyone likes to go fishing! Boys, girls, moms, dads and even grandparents like to fish. More than 50 million Americans fish. Fisheries managers are responsible for maintaining healthy and productive fish populations. But with so many anglers, this is not an easy job. More and more fisheries managers are starting to become "people managers" too!

What is good fishing to one person, may not be good fishing to another. Some anglers don't care what they catch as long as they catch something. Other anglers are only interested in a certain species of fish. Some want to catch lots of fish while others want big fish. Still others don't care if they catch anything as long as they get to relax in the beautiful outdoors.

MANAGING FISH POPULATIONS

A fishery manager must first consider the habitat in order to manage fish. As you have learned already, fish require the right water temperature, oxygen level, food source and cover. If you stocked a trout in warm water, you would be wasting the fish because it would not survive for very long. Likewise, if you put pike in a lake without vegetation, they wouldn't do very well either.

Most fish will spawn naturally and produce their own young. In these cases, a fishery manager does not have to stock fish every year. The fish replenish the waters on their own. A manager will then manage the fishery by improving the habitat, regulating the catch, and trying to balance the populations of fish species sharing the aquatic environment.

Hatcheries And Fish Stocking

Federal and state hatcheries raise many kinds of fish for stocking. Most hatcheries raise freshwater fish, but saltwater fish such as striped bass, red drum, salmon, snook, and sea trout are now being raised successfully. Fry, the smallest fish stocked, are the least costly to raise, but many of them die after release. Adult fish survive better but cost more to raise. Many states stock a combination of large and small fish in many lakes and rivers each year. States often stock trout

because they are fairly easy to raise, are good sport fish, and aren't as costly as other species.

Raising and stocking fish, however, is costly and sometimes not necessary. Why stock trout in a lake if the yellow perch fishing is great? Why risk upsetting the balance in a great bass lake by stocking northern pike? Fisheries managers realize that each lake or river has its own unique combination of fish present. This assortment of fish represents the "carrying capacity" of that aquatic system. Smart anglers know that if they sample different waters, they will discover a wide variety of fish. They also know that all of them are fun to catch and just about all of them are great to eat!

Certain fish populations, including sunfish, perch and bullheads, would benefit by more people fishing for them. Many anglers don't even know all these fish are out there waiting to be caught! Without enough angling pressure, panfish may overpopulate a lake or pond, resulting in lots of very small fish. This phenomenon, called "stunting" can be helped by anglers who take some of these panfish home to eat. More and more anglers are also discovering that these panfish can be the most delicious fish to eat! Refer to Chapter 3, Caring For Your Catch, to learn how to fillet these taste treats!

Managing Habitat

There are many ways to protect habitat for fish populations.

Aquatic plants are important for fish in most waters. They provide oxygen, attract food, and offer protection. However, too many plants are harmful and can "choke" a lake. Aquatic plants are hard to control. To manage weed growth, cutting, poisoning, uprooting excess plant growth and introducing fish that eat vegetation have all been tried. One of the best controls is limiting the plant food that enters the water in the form of sewage, fertilizers, or farm waste.

Building "artificial reefs" to attract and provide a home for both freshwater and saltwater fish is another way fisheries managers improve some fisheries. Such artificial habitat provides cover, safety, and food for fish. Artificial reefs can be as simple as sinking a weighted Christmas tree in a lake or as complex as sinking an old ship offshore in the ocean. Reefs are important because they provide an area for the bottom of the food chain to develop. The algae and plankton that develop there are a source of food for bait fish and for game fish. Also, many fish are attracted because the reefs provide them with cover. If you haven't guessed by now, reefs are good places for you to fish! However, always check with management authorities before attempting to put something in the water to attract fish. You may need a permit to place structures in a lake or stream.

Habitat Improvement

Working to improve water quality by reducing the amount of pollution entering the water is one of the best methods of improving fish habitat. State agencies make most of the efforts to improve habitat, but fishing clubs, scout troops, businesses, and local community groups supervised by state or federal fisheries people have helped on local projects too. Building small dams to raise the level of a pool of water, placing rocks or logs on banks to reduce soil erosion, organizing a stream clean-up effort, and building small reefs are projects that can be done in your area.

FISHING REGULATIONS

Modern fishing tackle, boats, and electronic equipment make it possible for anglers to catch many fish. People are also learning about fish and fishing by watching TV programs and reading books and magazines. Also, students like you study fishing and others attend special fishing courses. Because so many people are now learning how to fish skillfully, there's a danger that anglers may catch too may fish from some bodies of water.

Fishing laws or regulations protect the resource and help all anglers enjoy more success. The fact that most anglers must have fishing licenses is a common example of a fishing law or regulation. In most states, however, very young anglers and resident anglers of retirement age are not required to purchase a license.

Other regulations may:
- Set a limit on how many fish of a certain species you can take in one day.
- Set a starting and ending date for a fishing season.
- Set a limit on the number of fishing lines and hooks that you are allowed to use.
- Regulate the type of tackle and fishing method used.
- Set size limits for fish.

There are good reasons for such fishing laws. All are intended to conserve and improve fish populations. Often, fisheries biologists study bodies of water to check on fish numbers and the health of fish populations. Sometimes, they suggest a new law if it will help keep the fish population healthy. For example, if there is a fishing season in your state, it may have been introduced to protect fish during spawning or as a way of limiting the number of fish caught on heavily fished waters. Size limits are also meant to protect fish of spawning size before they are caught.

Some states have fishing laws that apply throughout the state. Other states may have different laws for different bodies of water. No matter where you fish, check the fishing regulations carefully before you fish.

Daily fish limits are meant to keep people from taking too many fish at one time. This makes it possible for more people to share in a fishery. Plus, they enable conservation officers to arrest "poachers" for stealing more than their fair share of the resource. You can help conservation officers protect your fish, forests, and wildlife by obeying the laws and reporting any violations that you see. Some states have a special telephone number for reporting fish and game violations.

FISHERY RESEARCH

Fisheries biologists are the scientists who manage fish populations. To do their job, they need as much information about a fishery as possible. They try to learn the needs of anglers and the condition of fish populations.

Biologists also need to know how many fish are being caught. They sometimes do this by taking information from anglers after a day of fishing. Sometimes, biologists study fish by collecting them with nets or in other ways. Biologists also mark fish with special tags or by clipping one or more of their fins. When marked fish are collected later, the biologists can learn many things. A tag or fin clip can tell them how fast fish are growing, how many are caught, and how far they have traveled.

After studying this information, biologists try to decide the best ways to produce more and better fishing for anglers while still conserving the resource.

FINANCING OUR AQUATIC RESOURCES

Do you know who pays for most of the research and other efforts to improve sport fisheries? Anglers do! The same people who use and enjoy them. Some money comes from the sale of fishing licenses and special-use stamps. Other money comes from a special government program. It's called the **Federal Aid in Sport Fish Restoration Program**. Some people also refer to

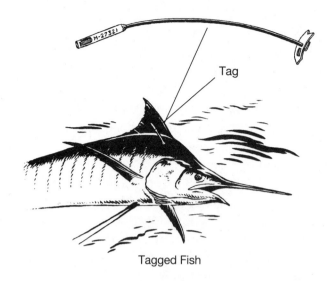

Tag

Tagged Fish

this program as "Dingell-Johnson" or "Wallop-Breaux." Here's how this government program works:

When an angler buys fishing tackle and a boater buys fuel, they each pay a tax that goes into a fund. Other money comes from the sale of tackle and boats imported from other countries. All of this money is then shared by the states to help pay for certain projects. The project may be building a public fishing pond or a large fish hatchery. The money can also be used to pay for managing fisheries, fisheries research, or for teaching people about the environment, conservation, water safety, and fishing. Each year, the Federal Aid in Sport Fish Restoration Program provides more than $200 million for such purposes.

Your purchase of hunting and fishing equipment and motorboat fuels supports Sport Fish Restoration and boating access facilities

YOUR ROLE

You can help those whose job it is to protect and improve our waters and fish populations. One way is to know and obey the laws for the waters you fish. You also can:

- Practice catch-and-release if you don't plan to eat a fish.
- If you catch a tagged or fin-clipped fish, you can report it to your state's natural resources agency.
- After fishing, leave the fishing spot cleaner than you found it.
- Never litter and do your best to remove any trash left by others.
- Get involved and support good conservation laws and programs.
- Teach others about our valuable aquatic resources and how to help conserve them.
- Report poachers to your local conservation officer.

Through your efforts, we will all have good places to fish for years to come!

ACTIVITIES

ACTIVITY 1 — LEARNING FISHING REGULATIONS

Obtain a copy of your state fishing regulations. Learn who needs a license, how to obtain a fishing license, and why a license is necessary. Identify the legal season opening and closing dates for different species, areas open to fishing, the legal methods for catching fish, and the size and number of fish permitted by law for several species. Notice that different lakes may have different regulations.

ACTIVITY 2 — DEVELOPING A CHART OF FISHING REGULATIONS

Make a list of five fish that you are interested in catching, and then make a chart with these topics:

Species of fish (your five choices)
Minimum length
Daily limit

Using your book of fishing regulations, fill in the data for your table.

This chart would be a welcome addition to the inside lid of your tackle box. Secure it well with tape so you can refer to it on your fishing trips.

ACTIVITY 3 — IMPROVE YOUR ANGLING WATERS

Contact your local chapter of a national or state organization involved in conservation and restoration projects. Volunteer to help this organization in projects involving fish stocking, tagging, or litter clean up, habitat improvement, or projects for the disabled.

ACTIVITY 4 — VISITING A FISH HATCHERY

Arrange a trip to a hatchery. Observe the methods and procedures necessary in the raising and stocking of fish. Find out what they feed the fish, how they keep the fish healthy, and how big they are when they are stocked.

ACTIVITY 5 — HOW MUCH MONEY IS SPENT ON AQUATIC RESOURCES?

Go to the library and find out how much money your state received last year from the Federal Aid in Sport Fish Restoration Program. You may have to ask a librarian to help you find the answer. Tell the librarian to look for the Wallop-Breaux Amendments to the Federal Aid in Sport Fish Restoration Act. Another way to find the answer is to write or call the federal aid coordinator at your state's natural resources agency or your local conservation officer. Also determine what projects these funds were spent on.

ACTIVITY 6 — WHAT LOCAL LAWS PROTECT US FROM POLLUTION?

Make a list of industries in your community that are next to a stream, river, or lake. Ask your local health department if there are special laws to protect these waters from potential pollution.

Fishing For A Career!

What do you want to be when you grow up? Many people would love to have a job that's related to fishing. There are many career opportunities for people interested in aquatic resources and the out-of-doors. Whether you're interested in teaching, biology, ecology, business, research, law enforcement, sales, writing, conservation, or various aspects of fishing, there is an option for you.

Federal, state and private agencies employ people with interests and skills in many of these job categories. Thirty-seven different federal agencies have some responsibility for managing the fish populations on their lands. Examples include the U.S. Forest Service, National Park Service, Bureau of Land Management, and the U.S. Army Corps of Engineers. Two federal agencies have federal authority for enforcing federal laws regarding the fishery. Basically, the U.S. Fish and Wildlife Service is in charge of freshwater and the National Marine Fisheries Service is in charge of saltwater.

THE U.S. FISH AND WILDLIFE SERVICE

The U.S. Fish and Wildlife Service is a federal government agency in the Department of the Interior. The Service manages a system of national wildlife refuges for migratory birds and a system of fish hatcheries and research areas in an effort to improve wildlife and fish resources.

The Fish and Wildlife Service is also responsible for enforcing several federal laws. These include the Endangered Species Act, the Marine Mammal Protection Act, and the Migratory Bird Treaty Act.

The Fish and Wildlife Service administers federal money to state governments, gives technical help to state and foreign governments, takes part in international meetings on wildlife conservation, and keeps the public informed about the condition of America's fish and wildlife resources.

THE NATIONAL MARINE FISHERIES SERVICE

The National Marine Fisheries Service is a federal government agency in the Department of Commerce. It provides management, research, and service for the protection of saltwater (marine) species. It also enforces the federal laws governing saltwater fish and mammals. This includes regulating both the taking of sport fish and commercially harvested living marine resources.

STATE NATURAL RESOURCES AGENCIES

The name of the state agency that deals with fisheries and wildlife varies from state to state. Some examples are: Department of Natural Resources; Department of Conservation; Department of Fish and Game; Game and Fish Commission; Department of Fisheries, Wildlife, and Environmental Law; and Department of Environmental Protection. You should find out what it is called in your state.

State Natural Resources Agencies protect and improve our waters and fisheries by:
1. Raising and stocking fish
2. Improving habitat for fish
3. Developing regulations to protect the resource
4. Conducting research on fish populations

5. Teaching citizens how to fish and to conserve resources
6. Using the media to keep the public informed
7. Building access sites to fishable areas

There are numerous employment opportunities in state natural resources agencies. Several of these are discussed below.

Fisheries Biologists

Each state and many federal agencies employ many fisheries biologists who help manage fish populations. Fisheries biologists must have an interest in biology, life sciences, and aquatic biology. Today, math, statistics, computer science, public speaking and writing are other areas biologists need to complete their science degree.

Fisheries biologists often work outdoors where they gather information and samples for study. This information helps them manage and conserve fish populations and protect the environment. They must have a good knowledge of fish and how they live. They also must know the interests of anglers and others who use the state's resources.

Law Enforcement Officers

State natural resources agencies enforce state laws designed to protect natural resources. The people who do this were once called fish and game wardens, but now some are called wildlife officers, conservation police, or law enforcement officers. Today, however, such officers do more than enforce laws that protect fish, forests, and wildlife. They also enforce environmental and pollution laws. In some states, they have the same authority as a state police officer.

Fish Hatchery Manager

People who raise fish in hatcheries or fish farms practice a skill called aquaculture. State hatcheries raise fish for stocking. Hatcheries raise everything from trout, bass, and catfish to striped bass and drum in both fresh and saltwater.

TEACHERS

Teachers who teach biology, ecology, and other sciences, including the study of fisheries, are needed at all educational levels. They may teach in the classroom or in the outdoors. Some may do research. Teachers need patience and a desire to work with young people.

CONSERVATION REPRESENTATIVES

Many non-profit groups are involved in the outdoors, including efforts related to fisheries. The Izaak Walton League of America, Trout Unlimited, the American Fishing Tackle Manufacturers Association, the Sport Fishing Institute, and the National Wildlife Federation, among others, are interested in our aquatic resources. These organizations have representatives who study laws and regulations, work to pass federal and state laws, represent anglers before the U.S. Congress and state governments, plan volunteer work, and publish newsletters and other materials to keep the public informed.

BUSINESS OPPORTUNITIES

If you think that you would like to go into business for yourself you have several options.

Tackle Shop Dealers

Tackle shop owners are in a field related to fishing, but their busiest times are when others are fishing. Tackle shop work involves long hours. Those selling live bait may open at 4 a.m. and close as late as 9 p.m. each day. A few may even be open 24 hours a day at certain times of the year. To be successful you must have a good business background and a knowledge of fishing and tackle.

Fishing Guides

You may know a fishing guide in your hometown. Guides provide boats, tackle, and fishing experience to paying customers. A successful guide must have the ability to locate fish, to get along with people, and a desire to take anglers to fishing areas and help them catch fish. Most guides work part-time and may have another job. For example, a teacher may guide on weekends or in the summer. Many tournament anglers began their careers as fishing guides.

Charter Boat Captains

Charter captains are much like fishing guides. They usually operate larger boats that hold six (charter boat license) or more (party boat license) paying customers. Charter boat captains must be licensed. Most operate their business along the seacoasts or on the Great Lakes. Charter boats range from about 20 to 55 feet in length. Some captains own their own boat; others operate them for their owners. Most charter captains have another job because they can't charter all year long. Some may move to another location to continue chartering year-round. For example, some Great Lakes charter captains travel south for the winter to work in warmer climates.

Commercial Fishermen

Commercial fishermen harvest fish to sell for food. They work with nets, traps, and long lines. The hours can be long and the work difficult and dangerous, especially in severe weather. When the fishing is good, the pay can be high. The work, however, is affected by many things, including government regulations, foreign imports, loss of fish stocks, pollution, breakdown of equipment, and poor economic conditions.

Fishing Tackle Manufacturer

Many people have begun tackle businesses with little money. They have started producing products in their home or garage for local sales, with some eventually building plants to produce and sell their products across the country. Today, some people start a small tackle business and succeed with good, new or unusual products.

Today, much fishing tackle is made in other countries and imported into the U.S. Some of the best jobs in the tackle industry are in areas related to the sale and marketing of tackle.

Manufacturer's Sales Representative

Tackle manufacturers depend on local or regional sales firms to sell their products to distributors and dealers. Sales representatives, often called "reps," own their own sales and marketing companies and contract with manufacturers to distribute tackle and equipment.

A sales rep is often responsible for selling in a number of states and must do a lot of traveling. A rep must enjoy meeting people, have good selling ability, and know fishing and fishing tackle. A good business education and experience in sales, promotion, or marketing are helpful.

PRINT AND BROADCAST MEDIA

Numerous career opportunities are open to you if you have an interest in journalism or radio or TV.

Outdoor Writers

Outdoor writers write about recreational activities. These include freshwater and saltwater fishing, hunting, camping, boating, hiking, canoeing, bird watching, photography, and skiing.

Many colleges have schools or offer courses in journalism. Most outdoor writers have a love of the outdoors and begin by writing and selling articles to state or regional magazines and newspapers. Some become full-time outdoor communicators with a large newspaper or national magazine. Others remain "free-lance" writers. Free-lance writers sell their written articles to a variety of newspapers or outdoor magazines or write books for publication.

Publishers

Publishers produce magazines, newspapers, newsletters, fishing annuals, regional and local guidebooks, and other publications. They are often in charge of the entire publication, including editorial and advertising workers. They also arrange the printing, distribution, and sales of the publications.

Broadcast Media

Many radio and television stations offer outdoor programs on fishing and other topics. These programs have become very popular. Some tournament and other well-known anglers have become the stars of these programs. The production of radio and television programs requires the talents of producers and directors, skilled technical people, cameramen, writers, and other specialists.

TOURNAMENT ANGLERS

A growing number of professional anglers are fishing tournaments for money. Very few of them, however, can make a sufficient full-time living from tournament winnings. Many receive endorsements from tackle manufacturers, conduct seminars at sport shows, and develop television or radio programs or video tapes on fishing. Even with these opportunities many professional anglers have other full-time jobs. Tournament angling is very competitive and demands a lot of angling skill, stamina, traveling, and sometimes luck to be successful.

OTHER CAREERS

There are many other careers related to fishing in some way. They include aquatic scientists for business, industry, and consulting firms; tour guides for local, state, and national parks and recreation areas; recreation specialists; research biologists; and environmental educators. College degrees are required for many of these jobs. There are many exciting and challenging careers waiting for you.

ACTIVITIES

ACTIVITY 1 — CAREERS EXPLORATION

Ask your teacher to invite one or more of the following people to class to discuss their job: fisheries biologist, conservation officer, representative of a non-profit conservation organization, tackle shop dealer, fishing guide or charter boat captain, outdoor writer or broadcaster, fishing tackle manufacturer, commercial fisherman, or a representative of any other job related to fishing.

ACTIVITY 2 — POSTER OF FISHING-RELATED JOBS

On the top of a piece of poster board, carefully title your poster: Jobs Related to Fishing. Show at least five jobs related to fishing that would be of interest to you. Find pictures in magazines and paste them on your poster board or draw and color them. Write the title for the jobs you have chosen under each picture.

ACTIVITY 3 — WRITING ABOUT ANGLING

Pretend that you are an outdoors writer and write a story about the outdoors that relates to angling, conservation, or some other topic of interest to you.

APPENDIX
B

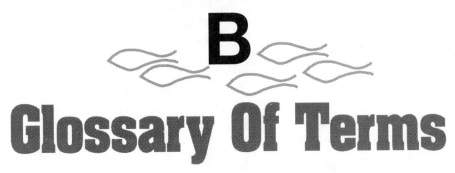

Glossary Of Terms

Acid Rain. Rain, dew, sleet, or snow that has become acidic from sulfur compounds in the air. Most acid rain comes from coal-burning factories and exhausts of autos.

Adipose Fin. The fatty fin on some species of fish such as catfish and bullheads.

Algae. Simple, tiny photosynthetic plants found in water.

Anadromous. Any species of fish that lives in saltwater and spawns in freshwater. Some examples are salmon, shad, and striped bass.

Anal Fin. The fin found on the lower portion of a fish's body near the tail.

Antireverse Lever. A lever or knob that prevents a reel handle from turning backwards as a fish tries to take line.

Backing. A soft, strong fishing line, such as braided dacron, that is wound onto a fly reel before fly line is added.

Backlash. Fishing line tangled on a casting reel; caused by the line spool continuing to turn after the line has stopped coming off the reel.

Bail. A wire device that spools the line onto an open-face spinning reel.

Baitcasting. The name given to casting tackle that uses a baitcasting reel; also called a "levelwind" reel.

Barb. The spur found on the point of most fish hooks. It is designed to help keep a fish from escaping from the hook.

Barbel. A whisker-like projection from the jaws of some fish such as a carp or catfish. Barbels help a fish to taste and feel.

Bass Boat. A boat designed for bass fishing.

Bobber. Also called a fishing "float" or "cork." It is designed to float on the water's surface and keep a bait or lure at a selected depth.

Bow. The forward part of a boat.

Buzzbait. A fishing lure designed to run on the surface. It has a large blade for creating a disturbance on the water's surface.

Cane Pole. Equipment that uses a long, slender rod and no reel; sometimes called a "bank pole."

Carnivore. A flesh-eating animal.

Catadromous. Any species of fish that lives in freshwater and spawns in saltwater, such as the eel.

Catfish. A group of fish without scales named for the long barbels around their mouths that look like the whiskers of a cat.

Caudal. Related to, or being a tail; the tail fin.

Chart. A "map" of water areas; shows shorelines, water depths, reefs, rocks, shoals, wrecks, and other areas of danger.

Charter Boat. A boat that is available for charter and can take out several passengers.

Cone. A cover on spincasting reels that prevents the line from coming off the spool during the cast. It protects the spool from dirt and grit; also called a "nose cone" or "reel cover."

Conservation. The wise use of a natural resource.

Cove. A small bay or inlet in a body of water.

Crankbait. Plug designed to dive to a certain depth as it is retrieved.

Creel. A fish basket or personal fish carrier used to carry fish when fishing on or near shore.

Creel Limit. A term to indicate the number of fish, by species, that can be caught legally in one day.

Current. Any movement of water, whether caused by tides, ocean water movements, or flowing water in rivers and streams.

Depthfinder. Also called fish finder or sonar; devices that signal the bottom and record it on a flashing dial, LCD screen, or graph paper.

Dissolved Oxygen. The oxygen mixed in water and used by fish; put into water by such things as wind, current, plants, and microorganisms.

DNR. Department of Natural Resources; abbreviation for the name of the natural resources agency in many states.

Dorsal Fin. A fin located on the back or uppermost part of a fish.

Downrigger. A fishing device used on boats that allows a troller to fish a lure at a precise, constant depth; a reel of heavy line or wire cable, a heavy weight to keep the cable taut, and a release clip for a fishing line. When a fish strikes a lure at the end of the fishing line, the line is released from the clip and heavy weight so an angler can fight a fish without any weight on the line.

Drag. A system in fishing reels that prevents a fish from taking line off a reel too quickly.

Drag Knob. The knob that allows the adjustment of the reel's drag pressure.

Dry Fly. A fishing fly tied to stiff hackle material that allows it to float and imitate an adult stage of a stream insect such as a mayfly, caddis fly, or stone fly.

Ecology. A branch of biology that studies the relations between organisms and their environment.

Ecosystem. A complex ecological community or environment forming a functioning whole.

Epilimnion. The warm layer of water above the thermocline.

Erosion. A process by which the surface of the earth is constantly worn away by the action of wind, water, and glaciers.

Estuary. A place where saltwater and freshwater mix, usually at a river mouth or in lagoons.

Ethics. A set of moral principles or values dealing with what is good and bad and with moral duty and obligation.

Eutrophic. A type of body of water that has high levels of nutrients.

Eye. The part of a fish hook where line is attached or where the hook is attached to a lure.

Fillet. Removing the boneless, edible part of a fish. It involves cutting out the flesh or muscle and usually then skinning the fish; the part of the fish cut out and ready to cook.

Fillet Knife. A knife with a long, thin, flexible blade used to fillet fish.

Fingerling. A young fish, about as long as the length of your finger.

Fisheries Management. The science of managing fish populations through research, habitat manipulation, stocking, water quality control and regulations.

Flasher. One type of depthfinder that uses blips of light on a circular dial to indicate the bottom and objects in the water.

Float. See "bobber."

Float Plan. Tells some person on land the boater's plans for the day and the expected time of return.

Fly. An artificial lure designed to look like an insect or small fish; made of fur, feathers, wool, tinsel, and other artificial materials; designed to be cast with a fly fishing outfit.

Food Chain. Also called a "food web" or "food cycle": the chain of organisms in a community that produce food and consume it; the path that food (materials and energy) takes through a group of organisms.

Freshwater. Water that contains little or no salt.

Fry. A method of cooking fish in hot oil; small fish that have just hatched out of the egg; after growing to several inches long they are called "fingerlings." See "fingerling."

Gaff. A "j" shaped, barbless hook on a long handle used to hook large fish while landing them.

Gill. A breathing organ located behind the gill cover on a fish's head.

Gill Net. A net that has a mesh size designed to catch fish by their gills, preventing them from escaping. Different mesh sizes are used to catch different-sized fish.

Gorge. A primitive type of fish hook. A length of stick, bone, flint, thorns, or other material that tapers to a point on each end. Some had a groove near the middle where a line was attached. The gorge was then inserted in bait. When swallowed and the line drawn tight, it lodged in the fish's gullet or throat.

Grip. That part of the rod held by the angler. Usually made of cork or a synthetic material.

Guide. One of the circular rings made of metal or artificial material attached to the shaft of a rod for the fishing line to travel through; someone who is hired to show a customer how and where to fish on a body of water.

Habitat. The place or type of site where a plant or animal normally lives.

Herbivore. A plant-eating animal.

Hip Boots. Waterproof boots that come up to the hips and are used by wading anglers.

Hull. That portion of a boat in contact with water.

Hypothermia. The rapid and abnormal chilling of the body. It can occur even in mild and warm weather. Victims must be warmed by special means to prevent greater or long-term damage or death.

IGFA. Abbreviation for the International Game Fish Association; a group that keeps records on fish catches and supports sport fishing.

Ice Auger. A large ice drill used to cut a hole in the ice for fishing.

Ichthyology. The branch of zoology that deals with fish, their classification, structure, habits, and life history.

Impoundment. A natural or manmade body of water.

Jig. A type of lure with a weighted head molded on a special type of hook. Often, rubber, plastic, feathers, and other materials are tied onto the shank of the hook.

Jigging. Fishing a lure, often a jig, while using an up-and-down motion with the rod.

Jonboat. A small boat, usually made of aluminum, with a square-shaped bow. It designed for use on calm waters or rivers. Jonboats range in length from about 8 to 16 feet.

Lateral Line System. A system of sense organs in fish; a series of pores or canals running along a line on each side of the body and on the head; detects pressure changes, including vibrations, in the water.

LCD. Abbreviation for Liquid-Crystal Display; a type of depthfinder that records its information on an LCD screen.

Leader. Any material used between the main fishing line and the hook or lure; can be made of monofilament or wire and be heavier or lighter than the fishing line. Often, a heavy leader is used to prevent fish with sharp teeth from breaking the line.

Levelwind. The part of a baitcasting reel that makes sure the fishing line is wound evenly onto the line spool.

Livewell. A container built into a boat for storing fish and keeping them alive.

Lure. Any artificial bait used to attract and catch fish.

Map. A drawing of land features. Maps are useful to find streams and access points to rivers and lakes. See "chart."

Marl. A type of bottom under a body of water; a mixture of clay and carbonate of lime.

Migration. The movement of animals, including fish, from one area to another.

Monofilament Line. A single, strong synthetic material used for fishing line.

Natural Bait. Bait that is found in nature, such as insects and worms, and common to a fish's habitat.

Net. A device used to capture fish.

Non-point-source Pollution. Pollution that enters water through run-off from land.

Nymph. A larval phase of an aquatic insect; an artificial fly tied to imitate a nymph; used primarily for trout fishing.

Olfactory Nerves. Nerves involved in the sense of smell.

Oligotrohpic. Lake type used to describe bodies of water characterized by low amounts of nutrients in proportion to their total volume of water.

Open Face. A spinning reel that has the spool uncovered or exposed.

Organism. Any living thing.

Oxygen. A gas that is necessary for all life, including fish life. In water, oxygen is in a dissolved form and is taken in by fish through their gills.

Panfish. A name given to small fish, such as bluegill, sunfish, and crappie, because they can fit in a frying pan.

Pectoral Fin. Either of the fins of a fish that corresponds to the forelimbs of a four-legged animal.

Pelvic Fin. One of the paired fins of a fish comparable to the hindlimbs of a four-legged animal.

PFD. Abbreviation for Personal Flotation Device; commonly called a "life vest."

pH. The hydrogen ion content, or the acidity or alkalinity of any substance. In water, most fish find neutral pH most comfortable. On a scale of 0 to 14, neutral is in the middle. A low pH means acidic water; high pH is caustic or alkaline. Either condition, in the extreme, can harm fish.

Photosynthesis. A chemical process that takes place inside cells. Light energy is used to make carbohydrates from carbon dioxide and water. A waste product is oxygen. The process is done by plants, including aquatic plants.

Population Density. The number of individuals of a given population occupying a unit of space. For example, the number of bass per acre.

Practice Plug. A weighted plug without hooks designed for use while practice casting with a fishing rod.

Predator. An animal, like a fish, that feeds on other organisms, including other fish.

Predator-prey. The relationship between a predator and that which it feeds on.

Pumping. A method of fighting fish that involves raising the rod to pull the fish closer, and then gaining line by reeling as the rod is lowered.

Push Button. A lever or knob on a spincast reel. Pressing the push button holds the line in place until pressure is released, at which time the line and lure can be cast.

Quarry. Prey; anything hunted.

Reading Water. The ability to look at a body of water and select the spots most likely to hold fish.

Redd. A nest dug on the bottom of a body of water by spawning fish.

Reel Body. The part of the reel that holds the gears and other controls.

Reel Foot. Reel part used to hold the reel on the rod. It is held by the reel seat.

Reel Seat. That part of a rod designed to grip a reel by the reel foot.

Reservoir. See "impoundment."

Retrieve. The act of rewinding fishing line onto a reel spool and retrieving a bait or lure.

Rigging. The process of setting up a fishing rod and attaching a bait or lure.

Rod Butt. The end of the rod handle.

Saltwater. Water with salt in it such as the ocean or the sea.

Sand Spike. A pointed hollow tube, usually of aluminum or plastic, designed to stick upright in sand to hold a surf rod.

Scale. One of the small covering plates on the body of many fish; removing scales from a fish's body before cooking; a device used to weigh fish.

School (of fish). A number of fish of the same species that are grouped together.

Scoring. A method of preparing fish by making narrow cuts almost all the way through, which allows hot oil to cook up the small bones.

Season. The period of time during the year that a particular fish can be harvested by an angler.

Sediment. The matter that settles to the bottom of a liquid such as water.

Sedimentation. The accumulation of sediment.

Setting the Hook. The act of embedding a hook in a fish's mouth.

Shank. The part of the hook between the eye and the bend, usually the longest part of a hook.

Sinker. A weight used to get or keep a bait or lure down in the water.

Skirted Spool. A type of spool found on open face spinning reels where a flange extends from the rear of the spool to cover the cup and spool housing.

Slough. A swampy place; marshy inlet.

Snag. An underwater structure that tends to cause a lure or bait to become hung up.

Snap Swivel. A small snap to connect lures or rigs to a fishing line that has a swivel to help prevent the line from twisting.

Snelled Hook. A hook that has a short length of leader tied to it.

Sonar. Another name for a depthfinder.

Spawn. The act of releasing eggs into the water by female fish for fertilization by male fish.

Spawning Run. The movement of fish to an area for the purpose of spawning.

Species. A biological classification of plants and animals.

Spinner. A standard lure that consists of a rotating blade on a shaft that holds a body or beads and ends with a hook.

Spinnerbait. A type of lure that has a jig-like head and hook molded onto a right-angle wire holding one or more spinner blades. There are single- and double-blade styles.

Spool. Device to store fishing line on any reel.

Spoon. A type of lure made of metal that is designed to look like a small fish.

Sport Fishing. Fishing for recreation, not for profit or commercial reasons.

Star Drag. A drag system consisting of several layers of soft and hard washers in a reel and controlled by a star-shaped wheel.

Steak. A chunk of fish that is made by cutting fish into steaks by transverse cuts through the body. Used for larger fish.

Stern. The rear end of a boat.

Stickbait. An artificial lure that floats and has no built-in action, but must be worked by the angler.

Still Fishing. Fishing in one spot and waiting for a fish to take the bait.

Streamer. A type of fly tied to a long shank hook, using feathers for the "wing" and designed to imitate a stream minnow.

Strike. The point at which a fish takes a bait or lure. Also known as "to strike" a fish; to set the hook.

Structure. A term anglers use for anything in the water that may attract fish. It includes rocks, weedbeds, stumps, piers, docks, and points of land. Structure can also mean any change, including type of bottom and water temperature.

Suspended Fish. Fish that hover considerably above the bottom in open water.

Swivel. A small fastener consisting of two eyes with a central barrel or swiveling portion. Designed for fastening lines and line/leader combinations to help prevent line twist through lure action.

Tack. A slanting or zig-zag course against the wind or waves.

Tackle. Fishing gear or equipment.

Tackle Balance. Term used to describe how a rod, reel, line, and bait or lure should be matched.

Tackle Box. A portable storage container for fishing tackle.

Tapered Leader. A leader used in fly fishing. Thick at one end it tapers to a thinner end, or tippet, the end where the fly is tied.

Taxidermy. Any of several methods of preserving fish for mounting as a trophy.

Terminal Tackle. The hooks, weights, snap swivels, and other tackle attached on or near the end of a fishing line.

Test. Line strength as stated on the label.

Thermocline. The layer of water where temperature rapidly changes from warmer water to colder water.

Transom. The rear of the boat; the portion onto which the motor is mounted.

Treble. A hook with three points used on many lures and for bait fishing.

Trolling. A method of fishing where lures or bait are trailed on the end of fishing line behind or to the side of a moving boat. This makes it possible to fish a large area rapidly.

Turbid. Not clear; muddy; cloudy.

Turnover. A very brief period when a lake is in turmoil. A mixing or "turning over" of the water takes place as cold water on the surface settles and water from below rises. This turnover homogenizes lakes that have stratified (layered according to water temperature) in summer and reoxygenates the water.

Ultralight. The name given to lightweight fishing tackle for casting small, lightweight lures.

Waders. A waterproof garment that covers an angler from the feet to the chest for wading in deeper water.

Watershed. The region drained by one river system.

Water Pollution. The contamination of water.

Weedless. A hook or lure that is designed to pass through aquatic vegetation without getting snagged.

Weight Forward Taper. A fly line with the heavy thick "belly" portion towards the front, with a front taper leading to the end to attach the leader, and a rear taper leading to a long line that is thin and takes little room on the reel.

Wet Fly. A fly that imitates an aquatic or land insect and sinks in the water; made of soft water absorbent materials.